*May this book inspire you to connect
with who you truly are.*

May you incorporate the practical steps to your daily life.

*May you approach each moment with
curiosity and compassion.*

*May you achieve the desired results
and fulfilment in your life.*

*May you take note of the infinite
possibilities that come your way.*

*May you be inspired to live your dream, and
live a legacy for generations to come.*

May you claim your ultimate potential.

YOUR TIME IS NOW

CLAIM YOUR ULTIMATE POTENTIAL

MARIANA ARDELEAN

Copyright © Mariana Ardelean 2020

Published by Empowering Strategies
PO Box 232
Rowville VIC 2178
Australia

www.empoweringstrategies.com.au

All rights reserved. Without limiting the rights under copyright reserved above, no part of this publication may be reproduced, stored in or introduced into a database and retrieval system or transmitted in any form or any means (electronic, mechanical, photocopying, recording or otherwise) without the prior written permission of both the owner of copyright and the above publishers.

Book cover design and formatting services by Self-publishingLab.com

First edition 2020

ISBN: 978-0-6484773-1-0 (print edition)
ISBN: 978-0-6484773-0-3 (ebook edition)
ISBN: 978-0-6484773-2-7 (audio edition)

For accompanying book resources and supporting materials, please visit www.yourtimeisnow.com.au

Contents

Acknowledgments vii
Foreword ix
Introduction 1
What Is Your Legacy? 5
What Do You Really Want? 29
The Importance of Goal Setting 49
SMART goals 77
The Power of Your Subconscious Mind 91
Functions of the Conscious Mind 101
Values 109
Moving-Towards Values 115
Moving-Away Values 127
The Power of Rules 141
Beliefs 153
Limiting Beliefs 165
Change Your Beliefs 179
Attitude 207
Standards 225
Success Practices 239
Sleep 245
Snooze Button 253

Set your intention for the day 261
Meditation 263
Visualisation 277
Affirmations 291
Exercise 303
Reading 311
Forgiveness 315
Gratitude and Appreciation 327
References 343
Notes 349

Acknowledgments

To my family, mentors, colleagues and friends, you know who you are. Thank you for standing by me, understanding me, and encouraging me to follow my dreams to pursue my passion.

Foreword

As someone who has read and written many books on personal development, business, leadership and self-discovery, I know how important they are, and how powerful they can be. Some books will guide you to external success—how to become smarter, wealthier, more productive—while others will take you on an incredible internal journey becoming your best self and living a happier life on your terms. Mariana's book is insightful and engaging in a deeper journey to becoming all you can be. She tells it like it is and she gets straight to the point. Her book will offer you principles, ideas and techniques that you can apply immediately to claim your ultimate potential and to create the success you want in life.

In reading this book, you will discover areas within your life that you may need or want to address. Once you have established which areas in your life need addressing, you can begin to make positive changes, to set goals and to work towards achieving them.

YOUR TIME IS NOW

Mariana will help you discover whether your life is imbalanced or not. She will teach you to have awareness, to understand and to appreciate the power of the subconscious mind. You will learn that, if you harness your subconscious mind, you are capable of achieving any goal, great or small, that you set yourself. You will come to understand the importance of your values, and that in knowing them will determine the quality of your life.

You will approach decision-making with more clarity and certainty. As your values are what guide you to make decisions, and your decisions are what determine your destiny.

Mariana's book will empower you to start challenging the beliefs that no longer serve you and the truths you currently accept that may be holding you back.

She will show you that your attitude and your standards are the things that lead you towards claiming your ultimate potential—and, as such, you should choose each of them wisely. This book highlights the importance of consistency and having daily practices that will set you up for success.

If you are reading this now, acknowledge yourself and where you are currently in your life: you are someone who desires change. You have already made a

FOREWORD

powerful decision because you have chosen to take the first step on a journey that will ultimately shape you into the person you wish to become. You are taking action towards achieving your goals, and that is no small feat. You have committed to yourself.

Get ready to engage and participate fully in your life's journey as you claim your ultimate potential.

I promise it's worth it.

You're worth it.

Sharon Pearson
Founder of The Coaching Institute
International bestselling author of seven books, including *Ultimate You*

Introduction

I would like to take a moment to acknowledge you for the simple fact that you picked up this book. This means that you are committed to yourself. You're committed to your journey to learn and grow, to implement new strategies and new practices, and to form new habits so you can achieve your desires and claim your ultimate potential.

In this book I encourage you to fast forward to the end of your life and ask yourself this question:

What will my family, friends, colleagues, and the members of my community say about me when I pass away?

This may sound alarming, but believe it or not it's very powerful. You are starting with the end in mind, and because you're asking yourself how you want to be remembered, this simple question will inspire you to create change in your life.

This book presents principles, strategies, exercises and tips for using those principles. I make no promise that it will be easy or quick; in fact, it will take time to dig deep and do the exercises.

YOUR TIME IS NOW

Be honest with yourself about where you are right now. Acknowledge yourself for that. Then take one step at a time towards claiming your ultimate potential.

This book is about acknowledging your current reality, becoming aware of your personal/professional life, and being able to make better decisions so you can develop a plan for your life.

If you have the feeling that you're out of balance; if you've become aware that your current circumstances are not sustainable long term; if you're making significant progress professionally, but neglecting your personal life; if you feel that life is too short; if you've been through trauma, either physical or emotional ... this book is for *YOU*.

The reality and the good news is that we all have more control over our lives then we realise. Unfortunately, most of us are not aware of that. By taking action, and taking the necessary steps, you can transform your life and claim your ultimate potential.

Within these pages, you will come to discover and understand how your mind works. You will also find out the things you must do on a regular basis to change your thinking, behaviour, and the way you approach any situation in order to achieve the results you're truly looking for in your life.

INTRODUCTION

To get the most benefit from this book, I recommend that you take your time working through it, and reflect. Get involved and do the exercises. This will allow you to think about what you really want in your life. Acknowledge your desires and think about where you see yourself in five, ten, fifteen or even twenty years' time.

It's only by knowing what you really want in life; understanding your conscious and unconscious mind; setting goals and intentions; understanding your attitude; knowing your values, beliefs and standards; and setting up daily practices that you will learn the secrets and step-by-step strategies to build your foundation. This knowledge is what you will need to reach any goal you set, in any area of your life.

You will begin to understand why most people are unable to reach their goals, or follow through on their plans. By appreciating the importance of consistent practices, and by implementing them as part of your daily routine, you will be able to see and recognise opportunities and possibilities that you were not noticing before.

By introducing daily practices and time for yourself, you will be able to look after your own wellbeing. You will also connect with yourself and everyone around you, rather than just with the technologies that are at your fingertips. You will plan your day, your week, your quarter and your year according to your desires, and the things you really love to be, do, have and give in your life.

Coming from a place of gratitude, and setting powerful intentions every day, will move you forward in your desired direction. This will set you up for fulfilment in your life because you will be able to achieve your desired outcome.

I trust that by the end of this book you'll be inspired to take the necessary steps to transform your life one day at a time, and to share what you've learned with others. As Ralph Waldo Emerson said, 'The only person you are destined to become is the person you decide to be.'

You are the expert when it comes to your life. When you start to look at every situation from a different perspective, you will begin to ask yourself if you're willing to look honestly at the deeper parts of you; the intuitive parts that will help you claim your ultimate potential.

And should you choose to go on this self-discovery, self-realisation journey, you will develop a sense of self-belief, self-respect, and self-love for who you truly are.

As Steve Jobs said in his legendary speech at Stanford, 'You can't connect the dots looking backwards. So you have to trust that the dots will somehow connect in your future.'

What Is Your Legacy?

*"Carve your name on hearts, not tombstones.
A legacy is etched into the minds of others
and the stories they share about you."*
—SHANNON L ALDER

When you start reading this book, find a quiet place where you will not be interrupted. Somewhere where you can clear your mind and let go of any worries about your family, work, business, friends, or appointments. Allow yourself to be open to the possibilities and opportunities that you would like to create in your life.

Without considering taking steps to plan your life, the chances are great that you will end up in an unfulfilled career, unhappy relationships with family, friends and colleagues. It could also lead to bad health.

The truth is that many of us spend more time planning a holiday than we do our own lives, we live without taking the time to stop, reflect and plan. This didn't occur to me until a few years ago, when I realised that nothing was going to change unless *I* changed. That's when I took the initiative and did something about it. I came to the realisation that it was time to plan and take charge of what I really wanted for my life, my family and myself. I thought about what I wanted to leave behind; what I wanted to be remembered for.

As a health professional, I work with and encounter many different people on a regular basis. I once had a patient who was a seventy-three-year-old man who was still working full time in a highly physical job. He shared a little about his life and why he was in this position. He told me that he was unable to retire because he couldn't survive on a pension.

Hearing his story made me reflect. I realised that without planning and looking into my own life, I could potentially end up just like this man, having to work late in life, not by choice but because I had to. I recognised that I didn't have a plan for my life; I only had a plan for my career.

WHAT IS YOUR LEGACY?

It's fine for those who want to work, who love to work, and who can work, but it can be very different for those who have to work in their later years because they are unable to pay their bills, buy food or even pay the rent.

Without planning, for most people, there is no choice. With planning, you are giving yourself choices. You can structure your day, week, quarter or year in such a way that you take care of what matters most to you in life. When you decide to plan your life and live the way you want with regard to the things you value the most—whether it's family, friends, career, hobbies or travel—you will feel in more control.

You can do this at any stage in your life, no matter the circumstances, by deciding to plan. It doesn't matter what age you are, or what position you are in. But the earlier you start planning, the better off you will be. As John Pierpont Morgan, one of the most powerful banking and finance legends of his era, said, 'The first step towards getting somewhere is to decide you're not going to stay where you are.'

What will your legacy be? What do you want to be remembered for? When most people think about legacies, they automatically think of material possessions, like a house or investments. A legacy can just as easily be the impact you have had on someone else's life. Indeed, it is the legacies connected to people that are the most precious. Years from now, what will matter most are the people—family, friends, and colleagues—that you have touched, even to the extent of adding value and profound meaning to their lives.

In one of her graduation speeches, Oprah Winfrey said, 'You're nothing if you're not the truth. The biggest reward is not financial benefits, though it's really good, you can get a lot of great shoes. Nothing wrong with great shoes. But those of you who have a lot of great shoes know that having great shoes and a closet full of shoes, or cars, or houses, or square footage, doesn't fill up your life. It doesn't. But living a life of substance can, substance through your service, your offering of your whole self. And the baseline for how do you live a life of a substance is whatever is the truth for you. What do you stand for? ... [Maya Angelou] said this, and I leave this with everyone in this room: "Your legacy is every life you've touched. Feel everything with love because every moment you are building your legacy."'

Oprah Winfrey is an example of what's possible when someone sets their mind to achieving a particular goal. She was born and raised in a poor family, and became the first African-American woman to host a television show. Oprah is seen as an icon, someone who is inspiring to millions of people across the world. She is someone who has paved

WHAT IS YOUR LEGACY?

the way for others to step into their greatness and become successful. She is a pioneer, and has often been the first to discuss on her show significant issues such as equal rights toward genders, racism, poverty, and other world-level topics.

Many people are so caught up in their day-to-day activities that they are too busy to stop and ask themselves an important question: *How is my life going to end if I stick to the same path I'm currently on?* Don't let this be you. Instead, imagine your life in the future, and how you would like it to be.

When you think about your legacy, you need to start with the end in mind. Many people don't do this; I certainly didn't. If you think about it, you'll realise that you plan most things with the end in mind. If you plan a holiday, first you choose the destination, and then you work backwards because the destination determines everything. How are you going to get there? Are you going to fly? Are you going to drive? What time of the year are you planning to travel? Will it be summer? Will it be winter? What kind of clothes will you take? Are you going to the beach, or are you going skiing?

The answers to these questions will determine what kinds of activities you choose to engage in. You know that if you don't plan your holiday well, you might not enjoy it as much as you want to. And this is the reason why most people spend a lot of time planning their holidays.

If planning a holiday is important, planning your life, starting with the end in mind, must surely be of equal, if not more, importance. Just as with a holiday, without planning your life, you may not reach your desired destination.

Political commentator Walter Lippmann said, 'The final test of a leader is that he leaves behind him in other men the conviction and the will to carry on.' If the people you leave behind are unable to do this, you haven't managed to pass on your legacy. We have all heard the saying, 'When the student is ready, the teacher will appear.'

Oprah Winfrey and many other successful people claim to owe their success to daily practices, and the one technique many uses is visualisation.

Visualisation exercise

Following is a visualisation exercise you will find helpful. You can either read the exercise as you lead yourself through it, read and record it for later use, ask someone else to read it for you, or download the audio file at www.yourtimeisnow.com.au.

Sit comfortably, either upright on a chair or on a cushion. And when you ready gently close your eyes. With your eyes closed, roll back your shoulders and lengthen your spine.

WHAT IS YOUR LEGACY?

Take a deep breath in and hold it … three … two … one … and breathe all the way out.

And again, take in a deep breath and hold it … three … two … one … and breathe all the way out.

And one more time, take a deep breath in and hold it … three … two … one … and breathe all the way out.

Imagine yourself waking up in front of a funeral parlour or perhaps a church. And as you walk forward, feel the ground underneath your feet. The door opens and you step inside. As you do, you notice the smell of the fresh flowers. I want you to listen to the soft music. It's familiar music that you love, nice and soft.

In your mind's eye, watch yourself walking down a long corridor. You come to a spacious room that has benches on both sides. You see people sitting on either side of you. You're looking at each person, but they're not looking back at you. Their heads are down. These people are familiar to you—they are your friends, family, old colleagues, others you haven't seen for a long time—but the look on their faces is unfamiliar. It's a look of reflection, a look of memory, a look of sorrow.

You think: What's happening? Why am I here? Why does everyone seem to be reminiscing and a little quieter than normal?

You walk to the front of the room and see a casket. You walk up to the casket. Not knowing who is in it, you

YOUR TIME IS NOW

come closer ... and closer ... and when you look inside the casket you come face to face with yourself. It's your casket, and this is your funeral.

On this day of your funeral, four people are going to speak. One is a family member. One is a friend. One is a colleague. The last is someone from your community. As you consider this scene, think about what each speaker would say about you and your life.

WHAT IS YOUR LEGACY?

YOUR TIME IS NOW

WHAT IS YOUR LEGACY?

YOUR TIME IS NOW

What kind of friend were you?

_____
_____
_____
_____
_____

What kind of family member were you?

_____
_____
_____
_____

What kind of colleague were you to work with?

_____
_____
_____
_____
_____

WHAT IS YOUR LEGACY?

What were you like to live next door to?

_____
_____
_____
_____
_____
_____

How were you at the supermarket?

_____
_____
_____
_____
_____
_____

How were you at the petrol station?

_____
_____
_____
_____
_____
_____

YOUR TIME IS NOW

How were you on holiday?

_____
_____
_____
_____
_____

How were you at family gatherings?

_____
_____
_____
_____
_____

How were you in a time of need?

_____
_____
_____
_____
_____

WHAT IS YOUR LEGACY?

How did you love?

_____
_____
_____
_____
_____

How did you forgive?

_____
_____
_____
_____
_____

How did you have fun?

_____
_____
_____
_____
_____

YOUR TIME IS NOW

How did you get back up when you fell down?

_____
_____
_____
_____
_____

How did you inspire the people who will speak at your funeral?

_____
_____
_____
_____
_____

What did you encourage them to do?

_____
_____
_____
_____
_____

WHAT IS YOUR LEGACY?

How would they say you changed their lives?

_____
_____
_____
_____
_____

What achievements and contributions do you want them to remember you for?

_____
_____
_____
_____
_____

What were you like as a mother, father, sister, brother, friend, colleague, neighbour or partner?

_____
_____
_____
_____
_____

YOUR TIME IS NOW

What do you really want to be remembered for? Think about something you haven't done yet and are keen to do.

WHAT IS YOUR LEGACY?

YOUR TIME IS NOW

WHAT IS YOUR LEGACY?

Now take a deep breath in … and breathe all the way out … relax. *That's* your legacy!

How do you feel after this powerful visualisation? Has it made you think about what you really want, and how you want to be remembered?

Every single day, you're writing your legacy. Every single moment, you're writing your legacy. During every single conversation, you're writing your legacy. In the way you live your life, through your experiences, and by the way you touch someone else's life, you're writing your legacy.

Your experiences are shaping your life and your life is shaping your legacy. Think about that: whether you realise it or not, you truly are creating your legacy in every single moment.

Your legacy includes everything you value in your life. Your beliefs and everything you embrace. The way you express yourself. The way you love. The kindness you show towards yourself and others. Your legacy is your spirit and your intellect, and this is what you pass on.

Every single one of us is creating a legacy.

The question is: What kind of legacy do you want to leave? Will you inspire and influence the people around you positively or negatively?

Your life matters. All of us are here for a reason, so you may want to consider what *your* reason is for being here.

YOUR TIME IS NOW

Dig deep. Be open with yourself so you can capture your true spirit. Engage your heart with your mind so you can connect with who you truly are. By connecting with who you truly are, you will shape your future and write your legacy.

Like the rest of us, you have no way of knowing how long you will be here for. You might be here for the next forty years. You might be here for the next ten years. You might be here for the next five years. You might be here for another day. You might be here for another moment. The truth is that none of us knows. But you can choose to make a difference, and you can start to do that by shaping your legacy now.

According to Steve Jobs, 'Almost everything — all external expectations, all pride, all fear of embarrassment or failure — these things just fall away in the face of death, leaving only what is truly important.'

Deep down in your heart, what do you really want to be remembered for?

Write your eulogy as if it were being read today. If you're like most people, you might find the process of writing your own eulogy a little unsettling. But the good news is that you're still alive, so you still have the power to change the way you choose to live your life and claim your ultimate potential.

WHAT IS YOUR LEGACY?

According to the Australian Bureau of Statistics if you were to take one hundred people at the age of twenty-five, in the same state of health and with the same level of wealth, and followed them for forty years, by the age of sixty-five their lives would look vastly different. One would have become wealthy, five would have become financially stable, sixteen would need to continue working, twenty-four would have died, and fifty-four would be dependent on welfare or charity, leaning on friends and family for financial support.

These statistics paint an ugly picture indeed. If we assume that none of these people planned to just 'get by' throughout their life, it means that a shocking ninety-four percent had not lived the life they desired, much less thought of leaving a legacy.

Having financial security is tied to a sense of freedom; the assumption is that you no longer need to be concerned about paying your bills if you have enough money. But financial lack is not the only problem society faces. Studies have confirmed that more prescription medications are consumed now than ever before; one in two marriages ends in divorce; most people have more debt than ever before; and serious health conditions like obesity, heart disease and cancer are all on the increase.

YOUR TIME IS NOW

Despite these statistics, however, every single one of us is more than capable of leading a fulfilling and happy life. It's possible for you to turn things around and claim your ultimate potential if you choose to do so.

Have you ever wondered that the way you think about your life might be the very thing that's preventing you from claiming your ultimate potential?

Most of us tend to make decisions based on our past. Because we believe that who we used to be is who we are now, our choices and decisions are limited by our past experiences. This means that when we come across new opportunities, we often turn them down on the grounds that we've never experienced them before. If someone cannot commit to their current partner because of a failed relationship in the past, they may be giving the current relationship the specific meaning they gave to the previous one.

Avoid the tendency that many people have to treat events in their lives as though they're disconnected from reality. If you feel the fear and act with strength— inner strength—every time you do so you will feel the greatness inside of you, and your confidence will grow. By taking one step at a time, you will be moving towards claiming your ultimate potential and leaving a legacy.

What Do You Really Want?

> *The starting point of all achievement is DESIRE. Keep this constantly in mind. Weak desire brings weak results. Just as a small fire makes a small amount of heat.*
> —**Napoleon Hill**

Only you can answer this question, and the more clarity and detail you include in your reply about what you really want—shaped by what you think, see, feel and know within your heart—the better off you will be. What do you truly love to be, do, have, and give in your life?

_____

_____

_____

_____

YOUR TIME IS NOW

YOUR TIME IS NOW

The more you can imagine; the easier it will be for you to see yourself being happy and fulfilled in all areas of your life, and the more likely you will be to claim your ultimate potential.

Every single human being is born into a state of disorientation. All other creatures are being guided by instinct; they don't question. Where's every single human being, on the other hand, has the power to examine and the ability to create their own life.

You can think and choose, and by doing this you can claim your ultimate potential. However, before you can change anything in your life, it's essential that you know where you are right now, and acknowledge yourself for it. Once you've acknowledged yourself, the next step is to have the desire to improve, learn and grow so you can change things in your life and claim your ultimate potential.

Knowing your current circumstances, and being aware of how to satisfy yourself in different areas of your life, is essential. Be sincere about it; make sure you measure, see, feel and know those things in your life that require your attention. You know the areas that you would like to improve as well as the areas in which you're happy.

WHAT DO YOU REALLY WANT?

Once you know your level of satisfaction in each area of your life, you will be able to see which areas to address first, which areas don't need to be addressed yet, and which areas can wait. As you do this, you will know what to prioritise. These areas can relate to your spiritual, mental, vocational, financial, familial, social and physical environment.

By identifying the areas of your life that you would like to start working on, you can measure your progress and take steps towards addressing those areas. This can be on either a personal or professional level.

Once you know where you're at in every area of your life, you can then decide what you would like to transform and concentrate on first in order to claim your ultimate potential and have balance in your life.

Why have balance?

Balance is about how you live and manage your life, as well as how you manage the relationships you have with everyone around you. When your life is out of balance, nothing seems to work or feel right. Finding just the right balance in your life, body and mind will help you achieve your goals.

When you know what you value, you can work towards achieving what you want a lot easier. Everything will feel effortless, and you will have a sense of fulfilment and satisfaction that strikes a balance in your journey toward finding lasting happiness in all areas of your life.

It's like yin and yang, with yin being passive and receptive, and yang being active and creative. They are opposite forces that complement each other. When you have problems in any area of your life, these two forces are battling against each other, but when you have balance in all areas of your life, everything feels smooth and effortless. If you have any areas of conflict—whether it's to do with your relationships, finance or health—it's because there is no harmony between yin and yang.

Wheel of life/balance

The wheel of life/balance is a fantastic tool that has been used throughout time. It's a very simple and effective tool for self-assessment. It measures your quality of life, and gives you an instant visual check of any area of your life that you may need to improve and pay attention to. This is beneficial in the sense that you'll be able to measure your progress and make changes when necessary, and

WHAT DO YOU REALLY WANT?

clearly see your level of satisfaction and fulfilment. This knowledge will give you a sense of satisfaction with your progress, and you will know you're working towards things that matter most to you.

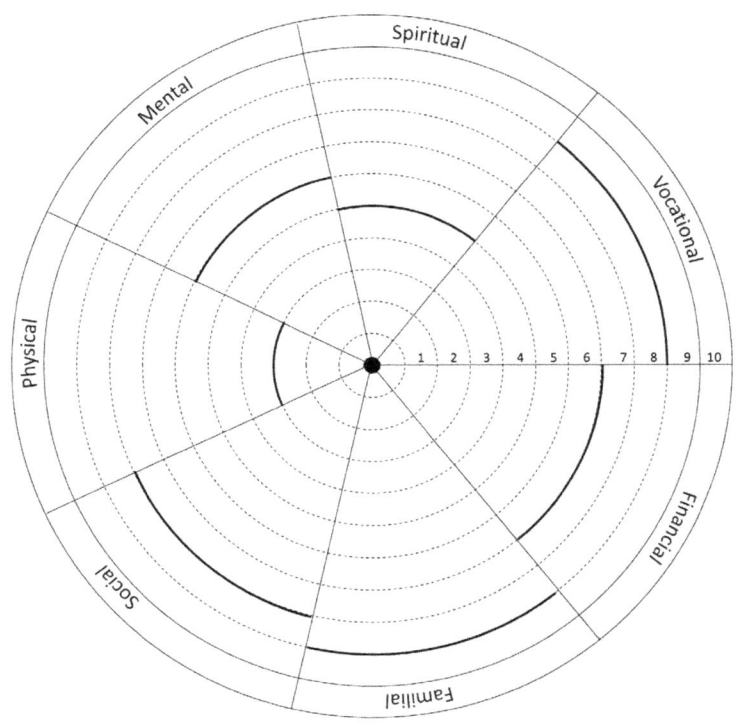

Wheel of life – Wheel of balance

Before you start doing the following exercise, it is essential to write down the date. This means that when you do the exercise again in three to six months' time, you can compare the results with the previous one to assess your progress.

As you can see from the diagram, the wheel of life/balance has seven areas: spiritual, mental, vocational, financial, familial, social, and physical. Satisfaction, fulfilment, progress and success are measured in levels 1 to 10.

Level 1 means you have no sense of achievement, fulfilment, growth or success in your life.

Level 10 means you are delighted with your progress and the way things are.

A line in the middle, at level 5, indicates average results. This is a sign of progress. This shows what is essential, and where you need to focus so you can improve your outcome. As you improve your outcome, the wheel of life gives you the sense of achievement and satisfaction that you're genuinely looking for in your life.

As you do the exercise, the important thing is to use the first numbers that come to your mind, what you *feel* is right. Use your intuition, not the number you think it should be, or the number you think is right. Your

WHAT DO YOU REALLY WANT?

unconscious mind will guide you, and you will know within yourself which level you're at in your life.

Balance in the wheel of life is a very personal thing and unique to each of us. What gives one person a sense of satisfaction and stability may be stressful or annoying for someone else.

Doing this exercise will raise your level of awareness and understanding, and you will be able to plan your life. You will be closer to what it means for you to have balance. This will help you clarify your priorities, and set specific goals in each area of your life. If you do the exercise at regular intervals, say every six to twelve months, you'll be able to see patterns that will help you understand and discover things about yourself.

It can be beneficial to ask someone else who knows you well to help you complete the exercise, someone with an objective perspective of your life balance. You may then start to see things from a different perspective as well. This person must be someone you trust and whose opinion you value, someone who does not have a hidden agenda and will be sincere in their responses.

Look at each area of the wheel of life/balance, and if you think something is missing or needs relabelling to make it more meaningful and appropriate for you, go ahead and make changes. The categories:

- Familial: label significant others, or people you are dating
- Vocational: label motherhood/fatherhood, work, business, volunteering
- Financial: label money or financial security or financial wellbeing.
- Spiritual: label higher self, centre self, religion
- Mental: label learning/thinking or self-development
- Social: label leisure or recreation
- Physical: label fitness, wellbeing or your environment in your home, workplace, career or business
- Additional categories: add any others you would like to include, e.g. leadership, community service, or anything else that applies to you and your life

After completing the exercise for the wheel of life/balance you will have an understanding of the areas in your life that you need to concentrate on.

Ask yourself when was the last time you were excited about something, so excited that you had the feeling you couldn't wait to share your excitement with someone else? I suggest you to think of something that makes you excited now because you are about to do a wheel of life/balance exercise.

WHAT DO YOU REALLY WANT?

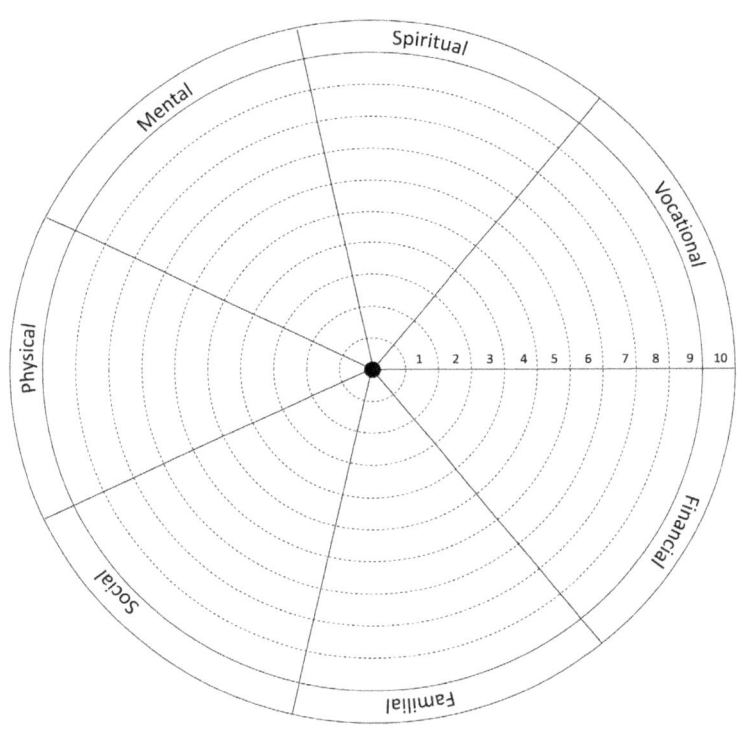

Wheel of life – Wheel of balance

Date: _____

Is this a bit of a bumpy ride? As you look at the wheel, you can delve into things a little deeper.

YOUR TIME IS NOW

Have there been any surprises? If so, what has surprised you the most?

_____
_____
_____
_____

As you look at your wheel, how do you feel about your life at the moment?

_____
_____
_____
_____
_____

How do you currently spend time in any of these areas?

_____
_____
_____
_____
_____

WHAT DO YOU REALLY WANT?

How would you like to spend time in any of these areas?

_____
_____
_____
_____
_____

What would give the area a score of 10?

_____
_____
_____
_____

What would the score of 10 look like and feel like for you?

_____
_____
_____
_____
_____

YOUR TIME IS NOW

Which of these categories would you most like to improve?

_____
_____
_____
_____

How could you create the space to make these changes in your life?

_____
_____
_____
_____

What help and support might you need from others to be able to make these changes in your life?

_____
_____
_____
_____

WHAT DO YOU REALLY WANT?

What lasting changes could you make?

_____
_____
_____
_____
_____

What changes are you committed to and want to make?

_____
_____
_____
_____
_____

If there were one action you could take, something that would bring everything into balance, what would it be?

_____
_____
_____
_____
_____

YOUR TIME IS NOW

Imagine that you could find a way to have a wheel where you experienced balance in all areas of your life. What would matter most to you? Imagine putting all your energy into it and being able to focus on the areas of your life that matter most to you.

_____
_____
_____
_____
_____

What would you be seeing?

_____
_____
_____
_____

How would you be feeling?

_____
_____
_____
_____

WHAT DO YOU REALLY WANT?

What would you be hearing?

What would your life look like?

What would you change?

YOUR TIME IS NOW

What would be different in your life?

_____
_____
_____
_____
_____

As you look at every area in the wheel of life, identify three areas that require action.

Three actions for: _____

_____
_____
_____
_____

Three actions for: _____

_____
_____
_____
_____
_____

WHAT DO YOU REALLY WANT?

Three actions for: _____

_____
_____
_____
_____

Now ask yourself these questions:

What do I want? Double-check: Is that what I want?

_____
_____
_____
_____
_____

What am I not paying enough attention to in my life right now?

_____
_____
_____
_____
_____

YOUR TIME IS NOW

What first step can I take right now that will point me in the direction of what I really want?

_____

_____

_____

_____

_____

Now is when you find out that the bumps you may be experiencing in your life are not because of the road. These bumps—the areas with a lower score—are where you need to concentrate and set some goals. Now is the time to balance your wheel, as you begin some goal setting in the next chapter.

The Importance of Goal Setting

*"Goal setting is the essence of life.
Tenaciously pursue your goals, not for
external praise but for inner reward. It makes
you a better person, parent, professional.
It is important to be constantly growing."*
—**Bob Proctor**

The importance of setting goals has been proven over the years. Without having clear goals and knowing the direction you want to go in, you will be unable to grow into the person you want to become.

Have you ever wondered how most successful people got to where they are today? Have you ever asked yourself how some of them managed to turn their lives around, from being the average person next door to becoming a multimillionaire, or even multibillionaire? The answer is simple: these people set goals for themselves.

One of the most famous and successful people of our current time, and also one of the wealthiest women in the world, is Oprah Winfrey, an African-American woman. In 2006 she was listed as one of the richest people in the world. She got to where she is today because she had goals, and the ambition to get there. Her achievement took time, passion, ambition, persistence, hard work and determination. She had to focus on her goals. She said, 'The big secret in life is there is no secret. Whatever your goal, you can get there if you're willing to work.'

What does Oprah Winfrey's example mean to you? If she could do it, it means that you can do it too.

You need to realise that most highly successful people are just like you. Whatever you see in them, you have within yourself. It's important to acknowledge that part of you. No one is born successful. You can become successful, too, once you've decided that it's possible. Once you have clear goals, you will be on the right path to success, which means you can claim your ultimate potential.

What exactly is a goal? According to the Merriam-Webster dictionary, a goal is 'something you are trying

THE IMPORTANCE OF GOAL SETTING

to do or achieve'. What exactly does this mean? It means that once you have a goal you will know exactly where you're going, and what you need to do to achieve the results you want in your life. Setting goals will give you a sense of what is possible. It can make your dreams a reality and boost your self-confidence because you will have something to look forward to.

In his book, *What They Don't Teach You in Harvard Business School*, Mark McCormack stresses how important it is to write down your goals. In 1979, Harvard asked their MBA (Master of Business Administration) graduates the following question: 'Have you set clear, written goals for your future and made plans to accomplish them?' The results were surprising. Only three percent of the graduates had written goals, 13 percent had unwritten goals, and the rest, 84 percent, did not have any specific goals.

The same graduates were followed for a decade and interviewed in 1989. The three percent who had clear written goals were earning ten times more than the rest of the graduates combined. The 13 percent who had unwritten goals were earning twice as much as the 84 percent that had not had any specific goals at all.

The way we think and what we believe can set us up for either success or failure. Also, it's important to understand the reason why some people get different results in their lives: 99.9 percent of people believe that if they *have* what they want, they will be able to *do* what they want, and that this will allow them to *be* what they wish to be.

To understand this better, you could say that once you *have* the perfect job you'll be able to *do* the things you want to do, and then you will become the person you need to *be*.

When someone comes from a place of *have, do, be*, their thinking is most likely in a state of want and need. They are probably not happy about their current situation and could possibly even sabotage themselves to get the desired outcome instead of being happy in the present moment.

Another example of this model of *have, do, be* focuses on money beliefs. Most people believe that once they *have* money they can *do* the things they want to do — such as save and pay their debts — and then they will *be* happy.

If you have this belief and this mindset, you're telling yourself that you're not content in the present moment, that you're not fulfilled where you are at, and that you won't be until you save money and pay off your debts. As long as you continue to think this way, you will

THE IMPORTANCE OF GOAL SETTING

probably never be happy because you will be chasing the things that you believe you need to have before you can be fulfilled.

On the other hand, successful people come from a place of *be, do, have, give*. They consider who they need to *be* in order to *do* the things they need to do so they can *have* their desired outcome and *give*.

By adopting this model of *be, do, have, give* and living it every day, you can focus on who you're being. You will be inspired to take the necessary steps and, as a result, have the things you want in your life.

It's essential to have a clear direction for your life and to set goals, otherwise you will go around and around in circles. You will waste a lot of time and be frustrated. It's likely that you will not achieve the expected results or fulfilment in your life.

It's like getting in your car to go to an appointment without having the address of where you're going. What would be the chances of you getting to your appointment? Without knowing the address, how could you?

Most people live their lives on autopilot, without clear goals or direction. Knowing what you would like to change in your life, setting clearly defined goals for each area of your life, and then taking action one step at the time will enable you to achieve and claim your ultimate potential.

> *Setting goals is the first step in turning the invisible into the visible.*
> —**Tony Robbins**

Before you consider setting a goal for yourself, it's important to set intentions. An intention is a long-term vision, for both your life and your future; it's the reason why you want to achieve your goals. An intention is an energetic statement about the outcome you envision. Your intention statement must be in the present tense.

At this stage, concentrate on your *why* and the reason you want to do things. Don't worry about the *how*, because that can change along the way. It's like when you set your GPS in your car or on your phone to take you to a specific address, and it gives you three different routes that will take you to the same destination.

An example of an intention statement: *I have all the money I need with plenty left over. I'm following my passion. I'm travelling, and spending time with my family and friends as well as donating to causes that I'm passionate about.*

THE IMPORTANCE OF GOAL SETTING

_____
_____
_____
_____
_____
_____
_____
_____
_____

Before you set your goals, take a look at your intention statement and contemplate for a moment. What goals would you set so you can arrive at your future vision and intention for yourself?

As Dr Wayne Dyer says, 'Our intention creates our reality.' Your intention statement is an energetic statement that describes what fulfilment feels and looks like in any area of your life, and describes those things that you want to create and change.

Work out exactly what you will be doing by setting your intention for the day. If you set a goal without a clear intention, without knowing the reason why you have set it, when you're faced with challenges in your life you will most likely lose interest and become

YOUR TIME IS NOW

discouraged, stop taking action, or even give up entirely on following through.

There is a story told about Albert Einstein. He was once travelling on a train when the conductor asked for his ticket. Einstein checked his jacket pocket. He couldn't find his ticket. He checked his trousers pockets. He couldn't find his ticket. He checked his briefcase. He was unable to see it there, either. Then he looked around the seat. He failed to find it there.

The conductor said to Einstein, 'Dr Einstein, I know who you are, we all know who you are, I'm sure you would have bought a ticket.' And he went on down the aisle, punching the tickets for the rest of the passengers.

When the conductor turned around, he saw Einstein down on his hands and knees, looking for his ticket under the seats. The conductor turned back and said, 'Dr Einstein, don't worry, I know who you are. No problem, you don't need a ticket. I'm sure you would have bought one.'

In that moment, Einstein looked back at him and said, 'Young man, I do know who I am. What I don't know is where I'm going.'

Even though the story may not have any validity, it does make us stop and think about where we are heading in our lives. Most people drift through life

THE IMPORTANCE OF GOAL SETTING

without having a particular destination or plan to realise their potential. Most people don't set goals or develop strategies for bringing fulfilment to their lives.

I certainly can relate to this. Until recently I had never written down my goals, and because of this I sometimes forgot I even had a goal, or it took me a lot longer to achieve what I wanted because I wasn't focusing on my goal.

Most people face life on a daily basis with apprehension because they don't have a well-designed plan. They're not thinking about their future, and are possibly enacting someone else's vision of how to live their life.

If you design and plan your future, then you will face that future with anticipation because you have created and planned your future results in advance. This means your future will be captured by your imagination, and it will have an enormous influence on you and your potential.

To be able to design your future just the way you want, you must have well-defined goals that will pull you forward and inspire you. The better you define and describe your goals, the harder you will work towards achieving them. Without having goals, you may settle for simply making a living because of everyday life necessities. Most likely you will settle for existence rather than living a life of substance as you claim your ultimate potential.

You have a choice. Either you choose simply to make a living, or you choose to design your life. You can plan and live your life exactly the way you want it. Mark Twain said, 'The secret of getting ahead is getting started. The secret of getting started is breaking your complex overwhelming risks into small manageable tasks and starting on the first one.'

Most people are smarter than their bank balances, but they may not know that they can choose to do things differently. They can decide to look at things from a different perspective, but are not aware that they can do that. They don't believe in themselves and their ability.

Some people may not have enough reasons to become more, to do more or to accomplish more. Some may have the intelligence, but because they don't have enough reasons they settle for what is instead of what could be. Life sometimes has a strange way of showing us the way if only we're inspired to look for it.

If you know what you desire, and you have a reason for that desire, you will find a way to get it. All the answers, methods, solutions and people you need to attract into your life will come to you. The books you need to read, the audiobooks you need to listen to, the

THE IMPORTANCE OF GOAL SETTING

seminars you need to attend, the mentors you need, all of these will appear once you start searching for them.

With current technology, all information is at your fingertips. If you have a good enough reason, you will find the way. You will find the answers you need to achieve your goals and claim your ultimate potential.

Every person has their own reasons for doing things. That's why every single person is unique in the way they see things, the way they feel, and the way they hear things. Some people may be motivated to do well because of their families. Some people do well because of who they are. Other people do well because of the people they choose to surround themselves with.

Some people may love the feeling of winning. Others may do something because of the joy they get from doing it, the satisfaction they get from doing something they feel passionate about. It's not always about the money. For some people it's the journey. It's the feeling they get when they achieve the desired result, and because they love what they do they also get paid well doing something they are passionate about.

As Jim Rohn famously said, 'You are the average of the five people that you spend the most time with.' So associate with people you can learn from, people who will encourage you and see the best in you, even if you may not be able to see it in yourself as yet.

Some people may desire to do well because they want to leave a legacy and be remembered for generations to come.

When Andrew Carnegie, the business magnate, philanthropist and one of the richest man in America, died in 1919, a handwritten note was found in his desk drawer. This note was addressed to himself, and written by Carnegie when he was young. The note contained his life goal: *I will spend the first half of my life earning a fortune and the second half of my life giving it all away.* And that's precisely what he did. How inspiring is that?

Find reasons that turn you on. Find reasons that drive you to become more. Find reasons to do more, have more, share more. Find reasons to do something unique. Find reasons to do something that you really love as you claim your ultimate potential.

According to the research done by psychology professor, Dr Gail Matthews, at the Dominican University of California, by simply writing down your goals you're 42 percent more likely to achieve them. Statistics have shown that only three percent of adults worldwide have written goals.

THE IMPORTANCE OF GOAL SETTING

Studies done at Yale and Harvard, over a period of twenty to thirty years, show that people with written goals earn ten times more than people without any goals at all.

Goal setting is straightforward. As you decide on each thing that you really want, write it down. While you're doing that, think about your life and what inspires you. Think about your answers to the following questions:

What gets you up in the morning?

_____
_____
_____
_____
_____

What keeps you up late at night?

_____
_____
_____
_____
_____

YOUR TIME IS NOW

What turns you on?

_____
_____
_____
_____
_____

Who do you want to be?

_____
_____
_____
_____
_____

What do you love to do?

_____
_____
_____
_____
_____

THE IMPORTANCE OF GOAL SETTING

What do you want to see?

_____
_____
_____
_____
_____

Where do you want to travel?

_____
_____
_____
_____
_____

What do you want to have?

_____
_____
_____
_____
_____

YOUR TIME IS NOW

What do you like to share?

_____
_____
_____
_____

What new skills do you want to learn?

_____
_____
_____
_____

What extraordinary things do you want to do?

_____
_____
_____
_____

THE IMPORTANCE OF GOAL SETTING

What do you love to do for fun?

_____
_____
_____
_____
_____

What is important to you?

_____
_____
_____
_____
_____

With whom do you love to share your experiences?

_____
_____
_____
_____
_____
_____

YOUR TIME IS NOW

What specific places do you want to visit?

_____
_____
_____
_____
_____

What habits do you need to drop?

_____
_____
_____
_____
_____

What habits do you want to acquire?

_____
_____
_____
_____
_____

THE IMPORTANCE OF GOAL SETTING

Who do you love to meet?

_____
_____
_____
_____
_____

Do you love a house on the beach? Where? How much time would you spend there?

_____
_____
_____
_____
_____

Do you love a house in the mountains? Where? How would that feel?

_____
_____
_____
_____
_____

YOUR TIME IS NOW

Do you love a house in the country? Where? How would that feel?

_____
_____
_____
_____
_____

Do you want to invest in property? Have you consider your options?

_____
_____
_____
_____
_____

Do you love to invest in shares? What would that give you?

_____
_____
_____
_____
_____

THE IMPORTANCE OF GOAL SETTING

Do you love to learn a new hobby? What would that be? How would you feel?

_____
_____
_____
_____
_____
_____
_____

Do you want to buy a new car and why?

_____
_____
_____
_____
_____

Do you love to become an artist? How would you Feel?

_____
_____
_____
_____

YOUR TIME IS NOW

What contribution do you love to make to your community?

_____
_____
_____
_____

What charity do you love to support?

_____
_____
_____
_____

Before you start working on your future, take a moment to acknowledge yourself for who and where you're right now, and what you have achieved so far. List seven things you have accomplished that you are proud of:

_____
_____
_____
_____

THE IMPORTANCE OF GOAL SETTING

To plan the next ten years, ask yourself:

Who do you really want to be?

_____
_____
_____
_____
_____

What do you want to see?

_____
_____
_____
_____
_____

What do you want to do?

_____
_____
_____
_____
_____

YOUR TIME IS NOW

What do you want to have in the next ten years?

THE IMPORTANCE OF GOAL SETTING

YOUR TIME IS NOW

Take a moment to reflect. This is not a list of things that you can get; it's a list of things you really, really want.

Imagine that everything will fall into place just the way you want, and that you can have anything you want in the next ten years. What would that be? These are not things you can imagine yourself acquiring or buying. It's not something you can learn, or something you can see. It has to be something you really, really want in the next ten years, and you don't yet know how to get it.

_____
_____
_____
_____
_____
_____
_____
_____
_____
_____
_____
_____
_____
_____
_____

THE IMPORTANCE OF GOAL SETTING

_____
_____
_____
_____
_____
_____
_____

As you look through the items in your list, rate each one with a number: 1 means you want that particular item within a year, 3 means you want it within three years, 5 means you want it within five years, and 10 means you want it within ten years.

Count how many one-year, three-year, five-year and ten-year goals you have, and make separate lists for each of those numbers. Keep in mind that we usually overestimate what we can do within a year, and underestimate what we can do in three or five years.

Once you know how many one-year goals you have, pick the three that are the most important to you and ask yourself: Why do you want this?

Do the same with the three-year, five-year and ten-year goals. Ask yourself why those three goals you've chosen in each group are so important to you and write down your answers.

YOUR TIME IS NOW

SMART goals

*It doesn't matter where you are coming from.
All that matters is where you are going.*
—**Brian Tracy**

It's SMART to set goals. The acronym SMART stands for:

- Specific
- Measurable
- Attractive
- Results focused
- Timeframe

Being able to develop sound goals is critical in managing and evaluating your progress. Knowing the structure and how to set SMART goals is important. As we unpack this a little bit further, you will understand how to set extraordinary goals for success and fulfilment in your life as you claim your ultimate potential. Brian Tracy also said, 'People with clear written goals accomplish far more in a short period of time than people without them could ever imagine.'

When you set SMART goals, you must answer these questions:

- **Why**: Do you have a specific reason? Do you have a specific purpose in accomplishing this goal?
- **Who**: Who will be involved in the accomplishment of this goal?
- **What**: What specifically do you want to accomplish?
- **Which**: What specific requirements do you have?
- **When**: What is the specific timeframe required to achieve this goal?

Now we'll look a little more deeply into the acronym SMART.

Specific: A specific goal must be written in a very simple way to identify precisely what you want to commit to in as much detail as you can master. A

SMART GOALS

specific goal has a greater chance of being achieved than a general goal. A specific goal is non-negotiable; it's something you plan for and put in your calendar.

Measurable: Establishing concrete criteria for measuring the progress towards the realisation of every single goal you set is very important. The thing is you can't manage what you don't measure. When you can measure and quantify your progress, you'll stay on the path towards the realisation of your desired destination. This means you'll reach your destination, and on the date you have set for that particular goal. A specific goal must be measurable to provide tangible evidence that you have achieved it. A goal statement is usually measured and specific since short-term measurements are often built into the goal as well.

Attractive: Once you identify the goals that are most important to you, goals that you desire, you will begin to figure out ways to achieve those goals. You will be able to develop your attitude, standards and skills, and your expectations of yourself sufficiently to attain the desired results and claim your ultimate potential.

You will begin to see things that previously you may have overlooked. You will be able to see possibilities and opportunities that will bring you closer to the attainment of your goal.

Your goal must also stretch you slightly. You must feel challenged by the goal. If you are not challenged, the goal you have set is not big enough. I challenge you to set a goal that is big enough to inspire and challenge you.

The goal must be defined well enough so you can identify and achieve it. To accomplish the goal, you must possess the appropriate knowledge and skills required to achieve the goal, or have the ability to organise a team of people around you to help you do that.

You will be able to achieve any goal if you plan each step wisely. Establish a timeframe that will allow you to carry out the goal step by step by step. The step-by-step approach will help you achieve a goal that might not have been possible without it. According to Abraham Maslow: 'If you plan on being anything less than you are capable of being, you will probably be unhappy all the days of your life.'

Results focus: A result-focus goal must represent an objective that you're willing and able to work towards. A goal must measure the outcome, not the activity. With every goal you set, it's important to show that you're making progress towards the realisation of that goal.

When you set up a significant goal that inspires you, you will most likely be motivated and eager to work towards its realisation. The larger the goal, the more you will think about it, and the greater your determination will be to work towards it. With a powerful enough *why*, you will find the *how* because you will be inspired from within to take action. You will read that book, make the time to study, and manage and reorganise the way you plan and think. If the goal is worth it to you, you will find a way. If it really matters to you, you will do whatever it takes to achieve the desired outcome. You will wake up early or go to bed late to improve your skills. You will enrol in a course. You will find a mentor to get the results you want and claim your ultimate potential.

Timeframe: A goal should be linked to a specific timeframe that will create a practical sense of urgency, which will result in a bit of tension between your current reality and the vision and intention that you set for yourself. Without that tension, the goal is unlikely to give you the outcome that you're looking for. Anchor your goal within a timeframe, for example, by June 30. By doing this, you will prompt your subconscious mind into action to start working towards your goal.

Writing down the goal, and going through the SMART-goal process is essential. You will be able to accomplish your goal if you define it clearly and concisely. Revising your goal is important if you want to make sure that it's clear.

YOUR TIME IS NOW

When you write down your goal, act as though you're placing an order to a supplier over the phone. Once the supplier receives the order, they will design your goal specifically, just the way you want it, and then deliver it to you. When you write your goal, make sure the goal is clear. If anyone reads it, will know what you want to accomplish, even a child.

SMART-goal questionnaire:

Specific: What will your goal accomplish? Why would you like to accomplish it?

_____
_____
_____
_____
_____
_____
_____
_____
_____
_____
_____

SMART GOALS

Measurable: How will you measure whether or not the goal has been reached? What steps do you need to take? What evidence do you need to have?

YOUR TIME IS NOW

Attractive: Do you have the necessary knowledge, attitude, skill, ability and resources to accomplish your goal? Will the goal challenge you without defeating you? Have others achieved similar goals successfully? Is it possible?

_____
_____
_____
_____
_____
_____
_____
_____
_____
_____
_____
_____
_____
_____
_____
_____
_____
_____

SMART GOALS

Results focus: What will the results of achieving the goal be? What is the purpose of the goal? What is the reason for the goal? What will the benefits be once you have accomplished this goal?

_____
_____
_____
_____
_____
_____
_____

Timeframe: When do you want to achieve this goal? Does the timeframe for this goal create a sense of urgency?

_____
_____
_____
_____
_____
_____
_____

Understanding your goals

Whether you accomplish your goal or not depends on your willingness to take action towards its attainment. As Pablo Picasso said, 'Action is the fundamental key to all success.'

You may ask what determines whether you take action towards your goals in the first place. How inspired, determined and passionate are you? Why are your goals so important to you?

Let's do a little exercise. Pick your top three goals and answer the questions below. Even though you may end up repeating some of the answers, keep answering them because the information you end up with will give you more clarity and focus. You will also be more inspired and motivated to work towards your goals. When the *why* is strong enough, the *how* will be taken care of along the way.

> *If you want to live a happy life, tie it to a goal, not to people or objects.*
> **—Albert Einstein**

SMART GOALS

```
┌─────────────────────────────────────────────┐
│ Write Goal Number 1 Here                    │
│ _____ │
└─────────────────────────────────────────────┘

┌─────────────────────────────────────────────┐
│ Why do you want this Goal? What does it give you? │
│ _____ │
└─────────────────────────────────────────────┘
                        ▼
┌─────────────────────────────────────────────┐
│ Why do you want that? What does that give you? │
│ _____ │
└─────────────────────────────────────────────┘
                        ▼
┌─────────────────────────────────────────────┐
│ Why do you want that? What does that give you? │
│ _____ │
└─────────────────────────────────────────────┘
                        ▼
┌─────────────────────────────────────────────┐
│ Why do you want that? What does that give you? │
│ _____ │
└─────────────────────────────────────────────┘
                        ▼
┌─────────────────────────────────────────────┐
│ What would this goal help you feel?         │
│ _____ │
└─────────────────────────────────────────────┘
```

YOUR TIME IS NOW

Write Goal Number 2 Here
_____

Why do you want this Goal? What does it give you?
_____

Why do you want that? What does that give you?
_____

Why do you want that? What does that give you?
_____

Why do you want that? What does that give you?
_____

What would this goal help you feel?
_____

SMART GOALS

Write Goal Number 3 Here
_____

⬇

Why do you want this Goal? What does it give you?
_____

⬇

Why do you want that? What does that give you?
_____

⬇

Why do you want that? What does that give you?
_____

⬇

Why do you want that? What does that give you?
_____

⬇

What would this goal help you feel?
_____

YOUR TIME IS NOW

"If a goal is worth it to you, you will find a way. If it matters to you, you will do whatever it takes to achieve the desired outcome."
—**Mariana Ardelean**

The Power of Your Subconscious Mind

Whatever we planned in our subconscious mind and nourish with repetition and emotions will one day become a reality.
—**Earl Nightingale**

Being aware of, understanding, knowing and appreciating the power of your subconscious mind effects how you look at things, especially what you believe you can bring into your life when it comes to health, wealth, happiness, love and joy.

Having an awareness of the infinite potential that you already possess, and the power of your subconscious mind means that you will be able to find solutions for every problem you have in your life.

Being open-minded, you will be able to receive new thoughts and new ideas. Even though they may sometimes be simple, they will work only if you implement and understand the principles by which your subconscious mind works. By applying these simple principles, you will be able to achieve your desired results and claim your ultimate potential.

A good analogy that illustrates the way the subconscious mind works is to compare it to a garden, where you are the gardener. You look after your garden, planting seeds of thoughts directly into your subconscious mind on a regular basis without being aware that you're doing it. Those seeds of thoughts form your habitual way of thinking.

Imagine that your subconscious mind is a bed of fertile soil where you can grow any plants you want, good or bad. You can plant flowers (positive thoughts) or weeds (negative thoughts), and both will flourish in the same way. Understanding this is essential. It means that you can choose your thoughts to get your desired outcome.

You can seed thoughts of health, love, prosperity, or anything else you desire in the garden of your mind. If you continue to plant those beautiful seeds of thoughts, you will harvest beautiful results accordingly. As you deposit seeds of thoughts into your subconscious mind—seeds that are in harmony with what you desire—you will apply the power of your subconscious mind to any problems or challenges you may come across.

Your thoughts and feelings will create the world within, and the world within will create the external world. Your inner world is the creative power. All the things you express in your outer world are created by your inner world. Either you realise this or not; you're doing it either consciously or subconsciously.

Knowing how your conscious and subconscious mind works, and understanding the interaction between the conscious and subconscious mind, you can transform your whole life. It sounds simple, but it's not always easy because your subconscious is very sensitive to your conscious thoughts.

We could equate the conscious mind to the captain on the bridge of a ship, and the crew in control of the engine as the subconscious mind. If the crew doesn't know where the ship is going, they must follow the captain's instructions. If the captain gives the crew the wrong instructions, they will steer the ship in the wrong direction and possibly end up on the rocks instead of the required destination.

The crew is simply obeying the captain's instructions. They never question the captain; they just follow his orders. In other words, your subconscious mind will take the orders you give it based on the conscious beliefs that your subconscious mind accepts as true.

Your subconscious mind controls 96–98 percent of your perception and behaviour, and you think in pictures and patents. Your subconscious mind is unable to tell the truth from a lie, and unable to distinguish if something is real or imagined. It believes that every single picture you see or imagine is totally real. Your subconscious mind is like a personal computer. It stores all your beliefs, memories and habits, and is connected to the field of infinite intelligence.

As Henry Ford said, 'Whether you think you can, or you think you can't—you're right.' So, if you say you can't, you will experience lack, and if you say you can, you will experience prosperity and abundance. The choice is yours. By choosing to change your thoughts, you will change your destiny and claim your ultimate potential.

From the moment you were born, or even before that, you have been bombarded by negative suggestions. Without knowing how to counter your negative emotions, you subconsciously accept them, and over the years bring them into being as experiences. As a child, you didn't know any better. You were helpless, especially when faced with suggestions from your parents or teachers, or anyone else who was important to you. Back then, you didn't even wonder about the mind. The conscious and subconscious were mysteries.

As an adult, you can choose. Being aware is the first step. Then you can choose effective autosuggestion, which means you can consciously change what was impressed on you in the past. Or you can choose negative autosuggestions, which will probably not change your life.

Any idea that has been fixed into your subconscious mind since you were born—through education, repetition, conditioning or any other significant impact in your life—will not change unless you choose to change it by consciously starting to do things differently.

The important thing to realise is that it doesn't matter what happens to you. What does matter is how you choose to respond to any given situation. How willing are you to create change? How willing are you to look at things from a different perspective?

Three levels of mind

The mind has three levels: conscious, subconscious, and unconscious. The conscious mind works on logic and reasoning. Below the conscious mind is the subconscious mind, and this is where the easily accessible information is found. If someone asked you for a phone number, you could probably retrieve it relatively easily. This type of information does not sit on your conscious mind; it exists in your subconscious mind and in your subconscious awareness, and you can retrieve it because you don't necessarily want or need to remember that information on a conscious level. You can access that information easily because it's information at your fingertips.

To give another example, you may be driving to work. Because you've been doing it for a while, it has become a habit. You know the direction, so your subconscious mind is helping you get there, even when your mind is preoccupied with something else. You might have a lot on your mind, and when you arrive at work you suddenly realise that you have no recollection of driving there. You weren't paying attention, you were thinking of something else, and yet you got to work safely. Your subconscious mind helped you get there.

THE POWER OF YOUR SUBCONSCIOUS MIND

Another example of your subconscious mind at work is when you are brushing your teeth. Most people do this in a specific order. They might pick up the toothbrush, then the toothpaste, and do it in this sequence every time. They're on autopilot; they don't have to think about it to be able to do it.

Your habits are stored in your subconscious mind, and it becomes second nature to do something without thinking about it because it happens automatically without the need for conscious thought. When your habits are ingrained, your body becomes your mind. The mind and body work together. The moment you begin to think, the way you feel and feel the way you think becomes your state of being. Your state of being is formed by your thoughts and feelings. Thoughts are the language of the brain and feelings are the language of the body. According to Dr Joe Dispenza, by the time we are thirty-five years old, 95 percent of what we do is memorised and our body knows better than our brain.

Another part of the mind is the unconscious mind, which is similar to the subconscious mind. It sits way deeper, and it's where you hold all information. It's like the foundation of your beliefs; your deep-seated emotions, which have been programmed since birth. This is the place where they first got stored. Once you decide to make any significant changes in your life, this is where the work starts.

The unconscious mind deals with the same things as the subconscious mind: habits, feelings, emotions, and behaviour. The difference between the two minds, however, is that the unconscious is the source of the information that your subconscious mind uses.

To understand the unconscious mind and what the unconscious mind might be thinking, it's helpful to think of the two minds as representing what you are aware of and what the actual reality is.

Let's say you want to lose weight. You think to yourself: *I can't wait to lose the weight. I think I'm going to lose it. I'm going to feel good when I lose the weight.* And so you feel happy, but for some reason you don't lose any weight. That's because you're sabotaging yourself.

Perhaps you ask yourself why you can't lose that weight. Possibly something happened when you were young, before you learned not to trust people. Or there could be other reasons to explain why you overeat, which effectively keeps you from having to deal with those reasons and those emotions. All this is happening on an unconscious level, and unless you're aware of what it is that's holding you back, you will probably not lose the weight.

THE POWER OF YOUR SUBCONSCIOUS MIND

Over the years there has been plenty of discussion over what is the right term—*subconscious* or *unconscious*. Unconscious is the term preferred by psychologists and psychiatrists since it refers to the thoughts that are 'out of reach' of our consciousness. (This should not be confused with the medical term *unconscious*, which means knocked out or anaesthetised; both definitions have similar qualities.)

The subconscious mind is easily accessible when you make a deliberate effort to recall something. The unconscious mind, however, is not as easily accessible. Any repressed traumatic memories, painful emotions, or recollections you don't wish to think about are stored in the unconscious mind.

It could be something traumatic, or something in the distant past: what you were wearing on your first day of school, or the name of your primary school teacher, for example. The memory is there, but you can't remember it no matter how hard you try. Specific psychoanalytical methods can bring back these memories (through hypnosis), or they can be triggered by a particular event, smell or touch.

In order to understand the mind better, we can start with the conscious mind.

YOUR TIME IS NOW

"Consciously choose to do things differently"
—Mariana Ardelean

Functions of the Conscious Mind

The key to success is to focus our conscious mind on things we desire, not things we fear.
—BRIAN TRACY

The conscious mind has four functions. The first function of the conscious mind is willpower. Let's take the example of a smoker who wants to quit. They may say, 'I'm not smoking anymore,' and the strength of their willpower will determine how long they last before the habit returns, especially when confronted with stressful situations in their life.

When the person says the words 'stop smoking', the unconscious mind only hears the word 'smoking'. This is because the unconscious mind does not have a concept for the negative. The chances of anyone being able to stop smoking without strong willpower and conscious thinking are very slim.

The second function of the conscious mind is temporary memory storage. This is the part you use on a regular basis for remembering things like family names and getting to work. These are the memories you use on a regular basis.

The third function of the conscious mind is analysis. This is when you consider a problem, analyse the problem, and look for a solution. This is part of the conscious mind, the part that makes thousands of decisions every day. Some of the decisions may seem to be automatic, but they are not. When you decide whether or not to do something, this part of your mind is where you make that decision.

The fourth function of the conscious mind is rational thinking. This part provides reasons for doing the things you do. In other words, for you to remain sane you must be able to rationalise your behaviour, even though that rationalisation may make sense to you alone and no one else.

To use the example of the smoker again, they may say that smoking relaxes them and calms their nerves, even though smoking is a stimulant and can't possibly

FUNCTIONS OF THE CONSCIOUS MIND

be used for relaxation. But those are the smoker's beliefs and that's how they rationalise smoking. If you believe something to be true, then it is true—for you.

The conscious mind also has the ability to focus, as well as imagine that which is not real. The language of the conscious mind is logic; however, the real you lives one level below the conscious mind, in the subconscious mind, where the emotions are found.

We all have habits that we display without even thinking, like answering the phone or getting dressed. It might be putting on our pants in a certain way, with the left leg first and then the right. These habits are automatic, something we do on a regular basis at a subconscious level.

This means that emotions—sadness, shame, anger, fear, hate—lodge in the subconscious mind. The logical conscious mind has no control over emotions. It's the subconscious mind that controls emotions, and this can cause problems.

Your subconscious mind holds your permanent memories. Everything that is happening in your life is recorded here: everything you see, hear or smell, and any feelings that you may have. All of these things sit on a subconscious level.

The memories that sit at a level deeper, in the unconscious mind, are anything that you don't want to access, such as trauma or unpleasant experiences.

The number one responsibility of the subconscious mind is to protect you.

The language of the subconscious mind is the imagination. And the communication between the conscious mind and subconscious mind is true picture.

The language of the conscious mind is logic, and the language of the subconscious mind is imagination, and when logic and imagination are in conflict the imagination will win every single time. What does this mean? It means that the subconscious mind is in charge.

Because the language of the subconscious mind is the imagination, it cannot tell the difference between what is real and what is not real. Everything is real to the imaginative mind; if it believes something is true then it is true.

The conscious mind is the watchman at the gate, and its function is to protect the subconscious mind from any false impression. The conscious mind is the thinking mind, where thoughts about ideas are rationalised, but it is really the subconscious mind that is in control.

FUNCTIONS OF THE CONSCIOUS MIND

For example, let's say you decide to go to the gym Monday to Friday. This is a conscious decision that you make. You may be able to use your willpower to get you to the gym for the first few days, but then all of a sudden you start meeting with internal resistance. You don't feel like going. You sleep through your alarm. Different things happen. You find excuses. All of this is the result of your subconscious mind.

Your subconscious mind is telling you, in that moment, that going to the gym is not normal. And because you don't want to do things that are not normal you decide not to do it anymore and you stop. But if you stick with it and go to the gym every single day, your subconscious programming would eventually be rewritten, and your subconscious mind would no longer be resistant to the idea of you going to the gym.

If you repeat actions often enough, again and again, you will eventually reprogram your subconscious mind and make those actions a reality. You will no longer have resistance. You can choose something consciously, but ultimately your subconscious mind will create the results.

You have the power to choose. You can choose health and happiness. You can choose to be friendly, or you can choose to be mean. You can choose to be cooperative, joyous, friendly and lovable, and the whole world will respond to you: you can choose to develop a wonderful personality. How you feel about your thoughts and images will be imprinted on a subconscious level, and your subconscious mind will create the reality of who you are—so you can change your actions and behaviour to create the reality you desire.

Your subconscious mind is connected to infinite intelligence. Your subconscious mind can reveal to you everything you need to know at every moment in time and point in space, provided you are open-minded and receptive.

The subconscious mind is responsible for healing the body; it regulates the body and knows the answer to all the body's problems. The subconscious mind does not judge or make decisions; it only responds to what's imprinted on, by the conscious mind.

Here is a list of negative statements you have undoubtedly come across that may hold you back:

- I'll fail.
- I haven't got a chance.
- It's no use.
- It's not what you know, but who you know.
- What's the use? Nobody cares.

FUNCTIONS OF THE CONSCIOUS MIND

- There's no point in trying so hard.
- I'm too old.
- I'm too young.
- Things are getting worse and worse.
- Life is an endless grind.
- Love is for the birds.
- I just can't win.
- Be careful you don't catch a terrible disease.
- I can't trust a soul.
- I can't.
- I'll never amount to anything.
- I don't want to look foolish.
- I need to be in control.
- I don't belong.
- I have to work hard.

YOUR TIME IS NOW

"You have the power to choose"
—MARIANA ARDELEAN

Values

*"It's not hard to make decisions once
you know what your values are."*
—**Roy E Disney**

Values are the things that are important to you, that you hold dear in your life. Collectively, they form a filter that influences what you focus on. Your values determine the quality of your life. Your values influence and determine all your decisions. And in turn, your decisions, and the choices you make, will determine your destiny. By knowing your values, you know who you are and what you stand for. Knowing what you stand for will determine the quality of your life.

Your decisions shape your destiny. The decisions you make on a daily basis are based on your values. Your values are associated with your worth, the meaning you give to your experiences and desires.

The same incident or experience will mean different things to different individuals in different cultures. What the incident represents depends on the individual's map of reality, and what they value and believe. For instance, in some cultures having lots of money might mean success while in other cultures too much money might be considered a risk.

This means that the meaning you attach to your experiences is the result of your beliefs and values. The experiences that you find most meaningful are the ones that are linked to your core values.

When you were growing up, you inherited values from your family, school, religion and culture. Understandably, you think that those are your current values, but that's because that's what you have been conditioned to believe.

All of us have values, regardless of whether we are aware of them or not. Most people like and admire others who stand for something and what they believe in. But the majority of people are not aware of their values, much less understand them, and how they shape and influence their lives.

VALUES

To achieve a sense of fulfilment and joy in your life, you need to have a sense of what's important to you and what you value. If you don't know what you value, you can't experience a sense of fulfilment and joy in your life. Your values are an internal compass, and act as a guide towards your ability to claim your ultimate potential.

Have you ever had a moment in your life when you were unable to make a decision because you didn't know what was important to you? In that moment you doubted yourself, which means that your values weren't met and you felt dissatisfied. If you know what's important to you and what you value, then you know what you stand for. If you know what you stand for, it will be easy to make decisions and commit to what you desire in your life. If you revise your beliefs and values, you can instantly change the meaning of your life experiences.

When you don't know what you stand for, you might find it challenging to commit and make decisions. When opportunities arise, you may not even see them, or the possibilities available to you, because you will filter them out, remove them from your awareness.

Whenever I meet a potential new client, I can easily tell if they will sign up or not. Most of the time it has nothing to do with our discussions. Even if they benefit from our conversations and have a shift in their thinking,

I know they will not sign on. I recognise the type of people who will not commit themselves, and in most cases it's because they don't stand for anything.

With this type of person, life just happens. And then they wonder why they're not making progress in most areas of their lives. They wonder why they're feeling frustrated, overwhelmed and anxious. They can't say yes and commit themselves because they have no idea what they want, what's important to them, or what they stand for.

The people who experience a feeling of fulfilment, satisfaction and joy in their lives are aware of what is important: knowing their values.

There are two types of value:

1 Means values
2 End values

Means values represent how we get there. They form the vehicle that we use to experience our emotional state, such as business, family, success, money, career, health, adventure and wealth.

End values are the emotions we desire to have on a consistent basis. When we discuss value in the context of claiming our ultimate potential so we can create an

VALUES

amazing life, we're referring to end values. End values include love, happiness, joy, commitment, persistence, passion, determination, and so on.

When you place importance on something, this means you value that thing. If you desire love, there are many different vehicles you can use to experience that value. The possibilities are endless. You have a range of options, with many different ways of experiencing this value.

Your true values are end values, and are moving-towards values.

YOUR TIME IS NOW

"*Your decisions shape your destiny.*"
—**Mariana Ardelean**

Moving-Towards Values

*"Try not to become a man of success,
but rather try to become a man of value.
Look around at how people want to get
more out of life than they put in. A man
of value will give more than he receives.
Be creative, but make sure that what you
create is not a curse for mankind."*
—**Albert Einstein**

Moving-towards values are pleasurable states that you value most and want to experience on a regular basis. In some cultures, people are influenced and pressured by their parents to follow a specific career path because it will give them status within their society, or to achieve a certain qualification, such as a medical or law degree, because they will earn more money.

I have come across many people in this situation, and they are often miserable because they are following a path that was chosen by their families and not themselves. Some rebel and do something else that they love instead, but many continue on the path that has been chosen for them without enjoying what they do.

Who are the most cherished and appreciated people in Western culture? In most cases they are people who know what they value and, most importantly, live their values and their standards; they do what they say they're going to do. We all admire people who stand for something and value what they do, because their values have an influence on society, even if we don't necessarily agree with their ideas.

Goals that you set for yourself are a noticeable expression of your values. What you value determines your strategies and your perception of particular situations. This in turn will determine your action or lack of action.

If you have a goal to increase revenue, most likely you value financial success.

If you value certainty, you will set totally different goals to someone else who values flexibility. As someone

MOVING-TOWARDS VALUES

who values certainty, you will set goals to give you that certainty. You may choose to work in a nine-to-five job, with a regular salary, well-established tasks and support around you. The person who values flexibility, on the other hand, will look for employment that suits their needs, with flexible hours and even the possibility of working remotely from home. Or they may choose to be self-employed.

If you value safety, you will constantly evaluate and assess any situation for potential 'threats'. Someone else who values fun, on the other hand, will assess the same situation, but instead be looking for any opportunity for entertainment.

Our values act as a powerful filter through which we see the world around us; they create our reality. Values are by definition subjective. Two individuals can have the same values but act differently in similar situations. Although they may share similar values—such as family, success, connection, gratitude, determination—they will have different evidence and criteria for assessing and judging particular situations. They will assess the situation to see if there is evidence and if their criteria are being met or not.

What values from the following list would you like to experience?

YOUR TIME IS NOW

Moving-towards values:

Abundance	Acceptance	Accomplishment
Achievement	Action	Actualisation
Adventurousness	Agreeableness	Ambition
Appreciation	Attractiveness	Balance
Beauty	Bravery	Calmness
Caring	Cheerfulness	Cleanliness
Comfort	Commitment	Compassion
Competence	Confidence	Connection
Consideration	Contribution	Cooperativeness
Courage	Creativity	Curiosity
Decisiveness	Determination	Discipline
Eagerness	Encouragement	Energy
Enthusiasm	Equality	Excitement
Exuberance	Faithfulness	Flexibility
Focus	Forgiveness	Freedom
Friendliness	Generosity	Genuineness
Gratitude	Gregariousness	Growth
Happiness	Helpfulness	Honesty
Honour	Hope	Independence
Inner Peace	Innovation	Integrity
Intimacy	Involvement	Joyfulness
Kindness	Leadership	Learning
Lovableness	Love	Loyalty
Magnificence	Masculinity	Meaning

MOVING-TOWARDS VALUES

Obedience	Open-Mindedness	Optimism
Organisation	Outcome	Passion
Peacefulness	Pioneering	Planning
Pleasure	Positivity	Power
Praise	Pride	Productivity
Purity	Purpose	Religiosity
Respect	Reward	Romance
Satisfaction	Security	Self-Awareness
Sensitivity	Sensuality	Serenity
Service	Sincerity	Softness
Spirituality	Supportiveness	Sustainability
Tact	Tenacity	Tenderness
Thoughtfulness	Tolerance	Trustworthiness
Understanding	Warmth	Wealth
Wellness	Wholeness	Wisdom

From the list above, choose between ten to fifteen values that resonate with you:

_____
_____
_____
_____

YOUR TIME IS NOW

Now take a moment to rearrange these moving-towards values in order of importance for you, starting with the emotion you would want to experience the most and finishing off with the emotion you would want to experience the least.

_____
_____
_____
_____
_____

Be more concerned with your character than your reputation, because your character is what you really are, while your reputation is merely what others think you are.
—John Wooden

Your values determine your motivation because they are integral to your identity. First come the 'I am' statements and then the values. Values determine the decisions you make and where you currently are in your life. They determine your results.

Some people may have conflicting values, for instance, valuing freedom but wanting results. Freedom

MOVING-TOWARDS VALUES

is a vehicle value; it's not a feeling. It's something you have rather than something you feel. If someone has freedom as a value it means they're not taking responsibility, and because of that they're not getting their desired results. Those who want results in their lives or their business must have freedom as a *goal*, not a *value*.

Someone who has freedom as a value will be experiencing challenge when it comes to making decisions in their life, or their business. Part of them wants to be free while the other part wants results. They will likely be unhappy, frustrated and overwhelmed, and will almost certainly not be achieving their anticipated results.

If you're clear about your values and what's important to you, you can begin to understand why you do the things you do: why you make certain decisions and what drives you. Start living your values if they are appropriate for what you want in your life. If they're not, then change them. Only then will you be able to achieve your anticipated results.

All behaviour is an adaptation to the environment in which we find ourselves, and the context in which we were raised—unless we become aware and are willing to change our environment and ourselves.

In what kind of environment were you raised? What kind of school did you go to? Was it a dictatorial environment or inclusive? Did you comply or did you rebel? Most of us are conditioned to obey the rules unless we make an active decision to rebel against them, even if it hurts us.

We are affected by everything that takes place from the moment we are conceived. Our imprint period, which is from nought to seven years of age, shapes our values on an unconscious level. During these years we are like sponges. We register everything that is taking place around us. This is the period when we absorb different patterns and emotions.

Following on from this is the modelling period, from seven to fourteen years of age, when we start to imitate our parents or someone we look up to, like a teacher.

Then comes the socialisation period, between the ages of fourteen and twenty-one, when we are most influenced by our peer groups. Normally we seek friends who are like-minded or who even look like us. During this period we can be influenced by the media. It's also when we start to have relationships and develop our social values.

From the age of twenty-one to thirty-five is the work-socialisation period, when our values are set unless we

MOVING-TOWARDS VALUES

are marked by a significant emotional event, such as the death of a loved one.

Some people believe that who we are and whom we associate with at around the age of ten determines our values, unless we delve more deeply and work to change our values. If you consider that period of your own life now, you may find that you have formed values that are not necessarily in line with what you desire in order to live a fulfilling life.

Most people, if asked what their top ten values were, would struggle to answer, let alone be able to place them in order of importance. Before considering your own values, it will be helpful to clarify your vision first. Ask yourself the following questions:

What kind of person do I want to become to claim my ultimate potential?

_____
_____
_____
_____
_____

YOUR TIME IS NOW

What do I want my life to be?

_____
_____
_____
_____
_____

What do I want my life to mean?

_____
_____
_____
_____
_____

What has been the most important thing in my life?

_____
_____
_____
_____
_____
_____
_____

MOVING-TOWARDS VALUES

What are my values, based on my present situation and the emotions I currently experience?

_____
_____
_____
_____
_____

Now ask yourself the following questions, which will help you understand what you will gain by having these values:

What values do I need to eliminate in order to achieve the results that I want and claim my ultimate potential?

_____
_____
_____
_____
_____
_____
_____
_____

YOUR TIME IS NOW

What values do I need to add to claim my ultimate potential?

_____
_____
_____
_____
_____

What do my highest values need to be to claim my ultimate potential?

_____
_____
_____
_____
_____

What order do my values need to be in to achieve the results that I want to claim my ultimate potential?

_____
_____
_____
_____
_____

Moving-Away Values

*" What you are afraid to do is a clear
indication of the next thing you need to do."*
—RALPH WALDO EMERSON

Most people talk about the need to be motivated to do something without realising that motivation is an external value. Inspiration, on the other hand, is an internal value. Motivation is when something has to happen for you to get moving; however, inspiration comes from within. If you're inspired, you don't need anyone else to motivate you. Instead, you will go ahead and do whatever it is without any prompting.

Moving-away values are often indicative of fear, although this is a generalisation. Moving-away values mean that you're unable to trust yourself or other people.

Respect is an interesting value. You're the only one who decides what respect means to you.

Moving-away values focus on the need for control and indicate a lack of trust in others because we can only trust ourselves.

> *Love is what we were born with.*
> *Fear is what we learned here.*
> **—Marianne Williamson**

Honesty, ethics and respect are all external-focus values. These values are designed to protect us from getting hurt. They represent the desire to be the checklist for the people around us, which is a form of control. Those who have these values are usually significance driven. They find connection with others difficult and prefer to connect through rules. Therefore, they have many rules around their values. They can also be disapproving of others.

If someone has many external values, it's likely that they have difficulty in connecting with their feelings because everything is external. This means they are driven, and have an external locus of control rather than an internal locus of control. What actually drives them is all out there—external—instead of internal.

MOVING-AWAY VALUES

If someone's values are external values, most likely they are driven by significance and certainty. Someone with internal values, by contrast, is keen to explore opportunities, is okay with failure, and is flexible in their thinking and behaviour.

If someone has a lot of external values, they are under the impression that whatever is happening around them is responsible for the way they feel; however, the truth is that they lose control. They are not in control because they cannot control a situation; they can only control how they feel about that situation.

> *Values are like fingerprints. Nobody's are the same, but you leave them all over everything you do.*
> —Elvis Presley

In the same way that we have emotional states that we want to experience on a regular basis, we also have emotional states that we would like to avoid. Most people do more to avoid pain and discomfort than they do to feel pleasure.

The thoughts that we associate with specific emotions influence and affect our decisions. This includes the way we look at things, the way we interact, and ultimately the way we feel.

Ask yourself and name some of the emotions and feelings that you want to avoid on a consistent basis. Do you know why you want to avoid them? We all have different reasons for wanting to avoid specific emotions. Having this awareness of yourself, and why you personally try to avoid certain situations, is important. In some circumstances, you may not want to put yourself out due to a fear of rejection or fear of being judged. Knowing this, you can understand why sometimes you self-sabotage because your values are in conflict.

Some people like to avoid feeling frustrated, humiliated, overwhelmed, angry, rejected, depressed, stressed, misunderstood or guilty, or even the feeling of procrastination. All these feelings are to some degree painful. For some people, some feelings are more painful than others, depending on the meaning they associate with them.

What values from the following list would you rather avoid feeling? Your answer will determine your behaviour and the decision you make in any given environment.

Moving-away values:

MOVING-AWAY VALUES

Abandonment	Anger	Annoyance
Anxiety	Apathy	Apprehension
Ashamed	Blame	Boredom
Cheating	Concern	Conflict
Complaining	Confusion	Contempt
Deception	Depression	Desolation
Despair	Disappointment	Disapproval
Discomfort	Disgrace	Dishonesty
Disillusionment	Disrespect	Distress
Embarrassment	Egotism	Exasperation
Exposure	Failure	Fear
Frustration	Fury	Grief
Guilt	Hate	Helplessness
Hopelessness	Hostility	Humiliation
Hurt	Incapability	Indecisiveness
Inhibition	Insecurity	Intimidation
Irritation	Jealousy	Loneliness
Loss	Mortification	Misery
Negativity	Neediness	Neglect
Nervousness	Offence	Panic
Powerlessness	Rage	Regret
Rejection	Remorse	Resentment
Sadness	Self-Consciousness	Self-Pity
Shyness	Sorrow	Stress
Shame	Tension	Terror

YOUR TIME IS NOW

Timidity	Unimportance	Vulnerability
Weakness	Worry	Worthlessness

From the list above, choose between ten to fifteen values that resonate with you:

_____

_____

_____

_____

_____

Take a moment to rearrange these moving-away values in order of importance for you, starting with the emotion you would do the most to avoid and finishing with the emotion you would do the least to avoid.

_____

_____

_____

_____

_____

_____

_____

MOVING-AWAY VALUES

As you reflect on your list, what does it tell you? Consider the emotion you have placed at the top of the list, the one you would do most to avoid.

Someone who places rejection at the top of their list could be avoiding situations where there is the possibility that they will be rejected. If they have listed rejection as their top moving-away value and success as their top moving-towards value, the chances of that person being successful are slim because they will do more to avoid rejection and pain than they will to gain pleasure.

To achieve success, we must be prepared to accept rejection. If someone is not interested in a product or service we offer and rejects it, we should not take that personally. The brain is designed to keep us safe and without pain, which means it will do anything to sabotage us and keep us safe before we become successful or even before we put ourselves in that position.

Some people may take two steps forward and one step back because their values are in conflict. Part of them wants to act and the other part doesn't because it wants to avoid the pain.

We all come across people who experience pain because of values conflict, and instead of criticism and judgement we would do better to ask ourselves why. The answer is that most of us have values that are in conflict within ourselves because we didn't choose those values. They were decided for us by the environment around us and our upbringing. Some may rebel and use alcohol, drugs or sex to attract attention as a cry for help.

Having awareness of your values is key to understanding and appreciating why you do the things you do, what drives you, and what may be holding you back. You can make a conscious decision about the values you need to have to achieve your ultimate potential. By changing your values, you can change your life, the way you think, the way you feel and the way you behave, and by doing that your whole life can change.

The other types of values are: values we leave, and values that we aspire to, such as freedom.

If you have freedom on your values list, especially if it's close to the top, you're probably not getting the results you want in your life or your business. Freedom is a goal and not a value because it's something to work towards and aspire to. It takes determination, commitment, tenacity, persistence and focus to get results. When you think of freedom as a value, you may be avoiding commitment. After all, freedom means being able to do what you want, when you want, with

MOVING-AWAY VALUES

whomever you want, and that often means avoiding responsibility.

We all have rules around our values. We can have easy rules so we can experience and live our values with ease, or we can have complicated rules. An example of an easy rule would be to experience freedom anytime we choose.

If you're not aware of your own rules around your values, it's likely that your values will be weighted towards moving-away as opposed to moving-towards values.

You earn your aspirational values by doing the work that needs to be done, and that means taking responsibility for your life. If you have freedom as a value but don't live it, your self-esteem will decline. This applies to all your values, but especially those that are in conflict.

> *Experience is not what happens to a man; it is what a man does with what happens to him.*
> —**Aldous Huxley**

If there is something you want but you don't actually live it, there will be a gap between where you are and where you want to be. This is known as cognitive dissonance. Possibly you will have filled this gap with lies, excuses, justifications, blame, avoidance and denial. The less you live your values the more cognitive dissonance you will have. The solution is that you must change your values or start leaving your current values behind.

This is why it's so important to build your inner self so you can turn to yourself instead of feeling the need to turn to external things to distract you and make you feel good about yourself.

> *Ask and it will be given to you;*
> *Seek and you will find; Knock, and*
> *the door will be open to you.*
> —MATTHEW 7:7

Those who are in business have freedom of choice. They can choose to do something or not to do something. They can choose to do that thing well or not well.

Values determine your up-front motivation, so if you have freedom as a value and try to build a business you will have conflict before you even start. Depending on the top values on your list, you might have challenges in your life, or even sabotage yourself. It is important to

MOVING-AWAY VALUES

be aware, have understanding, and know what really matters in your life. Do your values support you? Do you have clarity about why you do the things you do? Do you live in a way that is consistent with what you want and what you really value?

> *Not everything that counts can be counted and not everything that's counted truly counts.*
> —ALBERT EINSTEIN

Finding gratitude

Being grateful for where you currently are at in life and acknowledging that is an important step forward. Having gratitude only when things go your way will not build the qualities you want to have within yourself. Be grateful even when things don't go your way; look for the good that can come out of that situation.

You don't need to be grateful only for the things that you approve of. It's important to cultivate gratitude for every moment, even when things don't go your way. Find gratitude even when it's an inconvenience. In those moments, try to find *something* to be grateful for. It may not always be easy to find gratitude in each moment, but the more often you try, the more successful you will be. There may be moments when you think there's nothing to be grateful for, but if you look for the gratitude, you will be training your brain and neurology to be grateful even when things don't go your way.

It can be challenging at first. I certainly found it challenging initially, and still do. I know it takes time to adapt, and lots of practice, to be grateful on a regular basis. For some things in my life, I'm not grateful yet. I've worked hard to be grateful for those things I thought I could never be grateful for. I'm grateful now because those things have made me stronger, and more determined to challenge myself to look for answers, even when I thought at first that there are no answers. Looking back now, I know that I am where I am today because of this, and I'm grateful for that.

Acknowledge yourself for having a go instead of beating yourself up. Be grateful even when you think there's nothing to be grateful for. You may have things in your life that you're not grateful for, or at least not in that moment, but as long as you're working towards being grateful, you will find a way. Embrace what you're grateful for now, and acknowledge yourself for that.

MOVING-AWAY VALUES

Being clear about what's important in your life, and deciding to live your values regardless of the circumstances, is the only way for you to have fulfilment. In order for you to do this it's important to know what your values are.

Most of us know what we want (and this includes myself before I discovered the importance of values) without asking who it is we need to be first. Getting more stuff will not give you fulfilment. Only living your values and knowing what's important to you will do that, because your values are the compass that guides you to claim your ultimate potential. Your values are guiding you consistently to make decisions and take action to achieve what you want.

YOUR TIME IS NOW

"Decide to live in a way that is consistent with what you want and what you value"
—**Mariana Ardelean**

The Power of Rules

Your beliefs become your thoughts,
Your thoughts become your words,
Your words become your actions,
Your actions become your habits,
Your habits become your values,
Your values become your destiny.
—MAHATMA GANDHI

Now that you know your values, let's talk about the power of rules when it comes to those values, and the impact rules have when it comes to living your values on a consistent basis. First, ask yourself what rules you have for your values. A rule is a principle or a guideline that you must follow in order for you to meet a particular value, and to feel good about a specific situation or experience. This is your rule, and your belief.

YOUR TIME IS NOW

Your experience of a particular reality has nothing to do with the reality itself. This is because you interpret the reality through your beliefs, in particular the rules you have around what has to happen in order for you to feel good about a particular experience. These are specific beliefs that determine when you feel pleasure and when you feel pain.

Now ask yourself the following questions to determine what has to happen in order for you to feel happy:

Does someone have to tell me how much they love me?

_____

Does someone have to acknowledge me?

_____

Does someone have to appreciate me?

_____

THE POWER OF RULES

Do I have to make a six-figure income per year?

_____

Do I have to make a seven-figure income per year?

_____

Do I have to make six-figure income per quarter?

_____

Do I have to accomplish my goals?

_____

Do I have to drive a particular car?

_____

Do I have to be fit?

_____

Do I have to be healthy?

_____

Do I have to be well known?

_____

By reflecting on your answers, you will determine what has to happen for you to be happy. The reality, however, is that absolutely nothing has to happen in order for you to be happy. You can feel happy right now for no reason at all.

Consider this. If you make $20,000 per week, that in itself won't give you any pleasure. It is the *rules* that you have regarding earning $20,000 per week that give you pleasure.

You can send messages to your brain that change the biochemistry within your nervous system, causing you to have a feel-good sensation in your body. Your rules are external to you. If you structure your life and fulfilment around those rules, you won't have the ability to control certain situations, and the chance of experiencing pain will increase.

THE POWER OF RULES

Taking into consideration that your rules dictate how you respond in every single moment you're alive, it's imperative to know and set your own rules. Like many other things in your life, your rules have been determined by your upbringing, and the influences you've been exposed to in your life up to now. Your rules are shaped by the same system that shapes your values and beliefs. They arise from your cultural upbringing and conditioning. Someone born in Australia, for example, will have different rules to someone who was born in Asia or Europe or North America.

As you develop and start questioning and changing your values, you will start to question your beliefs and will continually develop your rules. As you grow into the person you want to become, you will delete, distort and generalise some of your previous rules, and develop new ones that will support you in where you're heading in your life.

Many people have inappropriate rules. Are your current rules appropriate? Are they going to support you in becoming the person you want to be? You may not realise this, but when you find yourself judging other people you are judging them according to your own set of rules, expecting them to conform to those rules. If you're easy on yourself, you're probably easy on others. If you're hard on yourself, you're probably hard on others, too.

It's important to have simple rules around your values so you can be flexible and are able to live them on a consistent basis. This will allow you to be happy any time you choose. If your rules are not simple and achievable, you will not feel that you are living by your values. The more rigid your rules, the more pain you will experience; and there is no room for flexibility where there is rigidity.

Your rules trigger your pain as well as your pleasure, and because of this it's imperative to have simple rules for your moving-towards values and inflexible rules for your moving-away values. Easy rules for moving-towards values will make it easier for you to experience and live your values on a consistent basis.

Many clients I work with have rules around their values that are very hard to live by on a consistent basis, which means they have to work harder to meet their values and often feel that they're not achieving what they set out to achieve. By having rigid rules, they set themselves up to fail and to self-sabotage.

Another thing to consider is that each rule has to be initiated by you. It has to be self-determined by you. *You* must control and influence your rules because the outside world does not determine your experiences. You do.

Examples of moving-towards rules:

Client value: love.

Complicated rules:

- When someone tells me they love me.
- When someone buys me a gift.
- When someone compliments me.

My client experienced pain because these rules were all external to her. She had no control over anyone else's behaviour, and what they said or did. If no one told her they loved her, she did not experience love. If she didn't receive gifts on a regular basis, she did not experience love. If she didn't receive compliments, she did not experience love.

After working together, however, her rules became simple enough for her to experience love consistently.

Examples of rules for moving-towards values:

Client's value: love.

Simple rules:

- Any time I choose to.
- Any time I talk with someone.

- Any time I breathe.

Take the time to put in place rules for every single one of your values.

Every time I [*insert action*] or any time I [*insert action*] or ... or ... or ...

Rules for moving-towards values

Ask yourself what has to happen for you to experience [*insert value*]:

Value one: _____

_____
_____
_____

Value two: _____

_____
_____
_____

THE POWER OF RULES

Value three: _____

_____
_____
_____

Value four: _____

_____
_____
_____

Value five: _____

_____
_____
_____

Example of rules for moving-away values:

Client's old value: rejection.

- I feel rejected when things don't go my way.
- I feel rejected when I'm not heard.
- I feel rejected when I'm not appreciated.

Client's new value: procrastination.
- I avoid on a regular basis being a perfectionist for myself as well as others.

Rules for moving-away values

Ask yourself what has to happen for you to experience [*insert value*]:

Value one: _____

_____
_____
_____

Value two: _____

_____
_____
_____

Value three: _____

_____
_____

THE POWER OF RULES

_____

Value four: _____

_____
_____
_____
_____

Value five: _____

_____
_____
_____
_____

Now that you have established the hierarchy for both the moving-towards and moving-away values and rules, ask yourself if your top value is going to encompass and support the rest of your values. Are these the values that will give you the outcome you need to live your dream and claim your ultimate potential?

Once you know what you value, it's important to commit and live those values on a daily basis.

YOUR TIME IS NOW

"The outside world does not determine your experiences. You do."
—**Mariana Ardelean**

Beliefs

> *There is a difference between WISHING
> for a thing and being READY to receive it.
> No one is ready for a thing until he believes
> he can acquire it. This state of mind must
> be BELIEF not mere hope or wish. Open-
> mindedness is essential for belief.*
>
> —NAPOLEON HILL

The *Oxford Dictionary* definition of a belief is to 'accept that (something) is true, especially without proof, trust,' or to 'hold (something) as an opinion; think'. In coaching, we say a belief is 'a convenient assumption'. One of the most important characteristics of human beings is that they build beliefs. Beliefs are what trap the majority of people in their problems.

Beliefs are usually unconscious assumptions that we make about ourselves, others and the world. Even though we can sometimes consciously think about our beliefs and may consider their validity, most of the time we don't challenge them.

Our beliefs have an influence on our sense of certainty, the content of our thoughts, our emotions and our behaviour.

You may ask how beliefs are formed. When we are born we have no beliefs whatsoever. We all arrive as clean canyases ready to be painted on. If a baby is born and lives in Australia, it will grow up having a certain set of beliefs. If a baby is born and lives in China, Europe, North America, Afghanistan, or any other far-reaching place on this planet, it will grow up having a different set of beliefs.

Every single one of us has a set of beliefs that is based on where we were born and where we live. Our beliefs, attitude, thoughts, feelings, memories, opinions and imagination create complex patterns in our brains, and our brain cells fire and release chemicals that represent specific sensory experiences called neurosignatures. Every single life event is associated with a specific and unique neurosignature. Our beliefs form part of the neurosignature of the adults that surround us as children. Just like downloading a program into a computer, our beliefs were downloaded into us, and we carry the opinions of those around us.

The beliefs are initially downloaded by our parents, and include not only what they say but also what they are like, what they do, and how they feel about themselves and the world around them. This ends up becoming part of our own installed belief system, and is added to by the other adults around us. They could be grandparents, other family members, teachers, other authority figures, and our peers.

Our names, languages, the places where we live, the schools we attend, and what we believe are all decided for us. As children, we accept this because we don't have a choice; our basic instinct compels us to follow and not be left behind, so we accept the judgements and beliefs of the adults around us as a survival mechanism.

What we observe about our environment is decided for us based on where we are born and the family we are born into. If the people around us have limiting beliefs, then we grow up with those same limiting beliefs. If we're told that we're not good at specific subjects in school, or don't play the piano well, the danger is that we will believe it. When we believe something, we search for evidence that supports that belief.

All of this means that what you experience is very different from what someone else experiences because everything has been filtered through your belief system. How you were raised, how you feel about certain situations, how you look at people from different cultures, and your thoughts about money all come from your environment. All of these things have been influenced by the belief system that you have carried with you, either consciously or unconsciously, since the day you were born. Dependent on your individual belief system, the world can seem happy, joyous and loving or full of fear, doubt and lack.

If two people are looking at a large dog, they will probably have two different opinions about that dog based on their belief systems. One person could see danger and be fearful of being attacked while the other could see protection and love. It depends entirely on the belief systems they are looking through.

By being aware of and understanding your beliefs, you can understand yourself better. Have you ever asked yourself how your beliefs influence your life? How you came to believe what you actually believe? Tony Robbins said, 'Beliefs have the power to create and the power to destroy. Human beings have the awesome ability to take any experience of their lives and create a meaning that

BELIEFS

disempowers them or one that can literally save their lives.'

Your personal beliefs are your guide, and as I stated earlier, they work as a filter. Your beliefs are the blueprint of your mind, and that's how you find meaning in and make sense of what's going on in your life.

In other words, your beliefs determine your daily reality. By understanding this, you will begin to see, feel and think because you'll be able to connect with your desired goals. What you would like to achieve in your life is closely connected to your beliefs and your values.

There are many types of beliefs, which we will now explore.

Global Beliefs

Global Beliefs are external beliefs about the different elements in our environment. Some examples of Global Beliefs are generalised statements that start with language such as:

- Men are …
- Women are …
- Relationships are …

- Tennis is …
- Success is …
- Sales are …

When it comes to Global Beliefs, it's important to be aware of them because they impact your personal life as well as your business environment. In business, employees, colleagues, suppliers and customers all have specific beliefs. For example:

- Social media is …
- Marketing is …
- Sales are …
- Culture is …

One of the most essential things to understand is that Global Beliefs can impact on the results you want to achieve in your life as well as in your business.

Identity Beliefs

Identity Beliefs convey a sense of self-belief, what we believe about ourselves in terms of our self-esteem, self-confidence, and who we think we are. Identify Beliefs form our close relationship with ourselves in terms of self-love and self-compassion, or the lack thereof.

Identity Beliefs are hardwired into the unconscious mind and they become our identity. As we journey through our lives these beliefs become our mask, our face to the world. The beliefs we create growing up determine our identity, and whether we see our identity as one of competence, passion, power and love, or worthlessness, incompetence and dependence.

When someone becomes immersed in a specific sport, cult or religion, they usually take on the traits that represent that specific world. Someone else who does not have those same interests could comment on them in such a way that seems offensive to the person involved, who takes it as though it were a personal attack. But the 'offensive comment' is only in the eye of the beholder. This can create a lot of hurt as it can put the person in conflict with those beliefs.

Values Beliefs

Values Beliefs are what we value and believe to be important in our lives versus what's not important to us.

Some people value family, some people value health, some people value fitness, some people value education, some people value wealth, some people value success, some people value fulfilment, some people value time, and so on.

What we value in life changes at different stages of our lives. Because of this, our priorities, experiences and values change as well. Values Beliefs influence our choices and the decisions we make, and this determines our ability to claim our ultimate potential.

Rules Belief

Rules Beliefs are the things we believe need to be present, in either our environment or our relationships, before we can experience our Values Beliefs.

An example of a rules belief: *You will exercise three times a week*. The days of the week are not specified, merely that you have to exercise three times every week. With this rule you have flexibility and thus the possibility of being able to sustain it long term.

Some people have rigid rules or too many rules around their values beliefs. For instance, they could say that no matter what happens they will exercise.

BELIEFS

Rules Belief need to be present in our minds in order for us to experience our values on a consistent basis, and to feel good about a specific situation or experience.

Spiritual Beliefs

Spiritual Beliefs are deep and powerful experiences. They enable us to confront any issues that we encounter in our lives. History tells us that Spiritual Beliefs are fundamental in all societies, no matter where that society is located and what religion the people believe in. They influence us in different ways and can bring peace and calmness into our lives because they mean we have faith. They may even raise questions regarding what we believe about life and what we believe about death.

Political Beliefs

Political Beliefs can affect all parts of our lives, since politics and governments exist everywhere. In Australia, we have national, state and local agencies that build and maintain infrastructure, such as the roads we use for transportation and engaging in commerce. Commerce brings economic prosperity into our lives. Many countries offer their citizens the freedom to vote and choose a particular party with a political agenda that they believe will make a difference. Political Beliefs deal with the kind of society we want to be a part of.

Education Beliefs

Education Beliefs are similar to political and spiritual beliefs. Some people believe in public education while others believe in private education. Some people believe that students who work hard in school and attain high scores will achieve financial success. That may not necessarily be true. People can become doctors or professors, hold high positions and earn a lot of money, and yet fail to become financially independent. The reason is often because they don't have a wealth mindset; they don't value wealth, they value knowledge. On the other hand, people who never finish high school, much less attend university, can become very successful and financially independent despite their apparent lack of education.

BELIEFS

Inherited Beliefs

Inherited Beliefs come from our parents or grandparents and are transferred to us when we are children and most susceptible. These beliefs have a considerable impact on how we think, our career choices, and sometimes even our relationships. In some cultures, parents encourage and influence, or even demand, that their children study to become doctors, lawyers or engineers. They do not consider their children's desires because they are more interested in the fact that these professions are respected and well paid.

As a parent, I have done this myself. At the time, I didn't realise the impact my actions would have on my family for the next ten years. By being a controlling mother and influencing my son's selection of his VCE subjects, a downward spiral began. I had thought that by choosing a variety of subjects—*not necessarily the ones that he wanted*—he would have more opportunities later in life. Halfway through his year-11 studies, my son dropped out of VCE. And so began the downward spiral.

YOUR TIME IS NOW

"Beliefs influence our choices and the decisions we make."
—**Mariana Ardelean**

Limiting Beliefs

> *You begin to fly when you let go of self-limiting beliefs and allow your mind and aspirations to raise to greater heights.*
> —**Brian Tracy**

So, where do limiting beliefs come from? Why do we believe what we believe? Taking into consideration that our beliefs drive our experiences, and that we rarely question our beliefs, we may consider that questioning our beliefs is a great place to start. I certainly did not question or challenge my beliefs for most of my life.

Since we are in control of our beliefs, and our beliefs control us, then this may be life's greatest puzzle. Our beliefs give us purpose, and every single one of us needs a purpose. However, if we wish to claim our ultimate potential and succeed in life, it's important that we question our beliefs, make changes in our lives, and connect our goals to our beliefs and values.

The way beliefs work is through the strength of the certainty of our words. For example, if we say, 'I'm positive I can,' we are certain of our efficacy. This particular statement has a specific energy, and it generates an attitude of power and the feeling that what we want is possible. When we believe in the words, the steps to get us there will follow; in other words, the *how* will take care of itself. When we believe that we can do something, we will do it.

On the other hand, if we believe that we can't do something, chances are we won't even attempt it.

If we have a strong belief, that belief triggers our unconscious mind to figure out ways and means of getting to the how-to process. If we believe and are confident, we generate positive energy, and others believe in us as we believe in ourselves.

Anyone can choose to believe and train themselves to see the good in everything, and this includes you. If you begin to seriously question your beliefs, you will likely find that many of them have no solid foundation. In fact, many of them may seem like ridiculous beliefs that you never even knew that you had.

LIMITING BELIEFS

Most people don't consider questioning their beliefs, and possibly you haven't either. As stated earlier, most of your beliefs have been inherited, passed down to you from generation to generation through your family, and also from teachers, your religion, and your culture. From the time you were conceived, you have been conditioned, genetically first and then environmentally to believe what you believe.

Unless you question your beliefs and choose to change those that do not serve you, you will struggle to claim your ultimate potential.

Sometimes you may hear people say, 'I just believe that …' or 'Can you believe that …' Some people become upset if their beliefs are questioned, but this is not necessary because most people have the freedom to believe whatever they want to believe.

I didn't believe in myself when I first came to Australia. I did not speak one word of English. Not speaking English was challenging; I used to ask my friend to come with me to the doctor's so she could translate for me. She was reading books in English, and when I looked at her I believed that I would never be able to read in English the way she did.

Fast forward. I am fortunate enough to have had some absolutely incredible friends, colleagues, and mentors over the years. Without them, I don't know what I would have done or where I would be today. Some of my friends and mentors believed in me before I believed in myself.

Surrounding yourself with people that lift you up and encourage you to do and be better is essential. It can make a difference in the way you think, the way you look at things, and the way you behave. Those who care about you will be sincere and give you feedback, which will enable you to consider how you can improve and make better choices so you can succeed in all areas of your life. Once you believe you can do it, you will do it.

Consider questioning your own beliefs. This is important, because it will give you a feeling of certainty, and knowledge of what a specific thing or situation means to you.

As an example, if someone has a belief that everyone is kind, compassionate and generous, they will experience those qualities in the people around them. Whereas if someone has the belief that everyone is mean and has no compassion, what do you think their experience will be?

It's important that you know what you believe, or, more importantly, what you *choose* to believe, as this will make a major difference in the quality of your life, your relationships, with yourself and others, and how

LIMITING BELIEFS

you experience the world around you as you claim your ultimate potential.

You have the ability to take and choose any experience in your life and give it a meaning that could empower you. You have the ability to choose and give meaning to the experiences that can disempower you.

Throughout history, there have always been people who chose to adopt new beliefs for themselves to empower themselves, and by doing this they also made the choice to help others. Perhaps someone lost a child, parent, or someone else close to them. They lived through a difficult circumstance that gave them the motivation to help other people and raise awareness so no one else had to suffer as they did. They were able to do this because they chose to believe in themselves, move on with their life and make a difference in someone else's life.

If one person can do it, we all have the ability to do it. We all have the ability to empower ourselves. Many people never know that it's possible to claim their ultimate potential by questioning their beliefs. They don't actually recognise that they have the ability to empower themselves—to choose, and to choose differently. As Albert Einstein said, 'Everybody is a genius. But if you judge a fish by its ability to climb a tree, it will live its whole life believing that it is stupid.'

You may experience an unexplained tragedy and circumstances in your life that take away your ability to have faith or belief in yourself. You ask yourself why this has happened to me. In those circumstances, it's important to find and have faith that something good will come from it, so you can empower yourself to move forward with your life and claim your ultimate potential. In those moments, ask yourself, 'What good can come out of this?'

An example of this is Victor E. Frankl, a psychiatrist who was a victim and survivor of the horror of the Holocaust and the concentration camps. In his book, *Man's Search for Meaning*, Frankl shares his belief that there is greater 'meaning in suffering' and that this can provide meaning and empower us to look at things from a different perspective. Many of those who suffered and survived the concentration camps were able to tell their stories and do what they could to ensure that their experience would never happen again to another human being.

Some of your beliefs will empower you and give you the support you need to be successful so you can achieve all that you want. Other beliefs may be holding you back, sometimes even to the point of sabotaging yourself.

Sharpening your awareness will sharpen your attention because you will be surrounded by billions

LIMITING BELIEFS

of constant sensory inputs: visual, kinaesthetic and auditory. It's important to know how to point your attention in the right direction since you can easily miss opportunities if you can't see what you're looking for.

Most of the time you will be looking for what you believe in, and this is known as the *reticular activating system* (RAS). At the base of the skull there is a bundle of nerve cells in the brainstem, and the main responsibility of the nerves is to filter out unnecessary information to make sure that you don't go insane with all the sensory input that comes your way. This is what keeps you alive, monitors your attention, focuses your goals, and regulates your alertness as well as your sleep-wake transition. The RAS is constantly filtering out and discarding information that doesn't match your current belief system.

Take the experience of buying a new car that is a bit different from the car you would normally buy. You may initially think it's uncommon and that not many people have one like it. Then the first time you drive the car it seems like everyone on the road has the same vehicle. Why does this common phenomenon happen? The reality is that those cars have always been on the road, but you didn't see them because you were not looking for them.

This attitude could be stopping you from claiming your ultimate potential. You may not be able to reach it because you can't see the opportunities, potential and possibilities. This could be affecting your chances of progress, intimacy, wealth, happiness and fulfilment. It could be preventing you from applying for the position you really want.

These are your limiting beliefs, and your limiting beliefs are being continually and perpetually reinforced. That's why they can be difficult to break. On a regular basis you interpret all the information that is coming to your senses, and you mould that information to fit the way you want the world to be, which is not always the way the world actually is.

This process of continually reinforcing and seeking what you like to see (RAS) is also known as *belief confirmation*. You're looking for evidence to reinforce your beliefs. If you believe that things are difficult or that the economy is bad, you will continue to see and reinforce that belief. That is all you will see. If the self-talk in your head is 'I'm not good enough' or 'I can't do this' or 'No one has trust in what I have to say' or 'No one likes me', that will continue to be your field of reality.

The thing you're doing in this process is called confirmation bias. This is when you filter and ignore

LIMITING BELIEFS

any information that contradicts what you believe. Take a political debate, for example. Most people are familiar with political figures that simply can't hear their opponent's argument because it contradicts their own view. They might concede a couple of points that confirm what they already believe, but that's only because that's all they can recall.

This process of recalling can be dangerous because it takes selected memories and treats them as proof. It's like going back to the past and selecting events that confirm your negative belief about yourself. If you believe you're not smart, you go back through your past and select instances that support that belief, and seem to support your argument.

Maybe you have made changes and are making progress, but then a stressful event comes along and you revert to your old pattern of belief. What this means is that the longer you have held onto those old belief systems, the deeper the roots have grown, and the harder it will be to extract those beliefs and replace them with new ones. When this happens, you must believe that you need to take your life in the direction that you want so you can claim your ultimate potential.

Some indications of limiting beliefs:

- That always happens.
- I never get it right.
- This won't work.
- This is hard.
- Why can't I do it?
- This should happen.
- Try ...

To find out what your beliefs are, be aware of the language you use. If you say, 'I always' or 'I never' or 'I can't', those words are probably covering up a limiting belief.

Main categories of limiting beliefs

Limiting beliefs fall into three main categories:

1 **Hopelessness**
   With this type of belief, you see the opportunity and become excited. You might want to do something, but you don't do it. Instead, you make excuses for why it won't work, perhaps claiming that you've heard it's just one of those things, or that someone you know tried it and it didn't work for them.

LIMITING BELIEFS

- It won't happen to me.
- There's no use trying.
- This is for other people, not me.

2 **Helplessness**

With this type of belief, you might have a go but when you run into obstacles your fear is confirmed and you quit.

- I don't have the ability.
- I'm not smart enough.
- I'm not talented enough.
- I don't have the right experience.

3 **Worthlessness**

This type of belief is the most important. Perhaps in your childhood your heart was broken, or someone made you feel worthless, as if you were not good enough. You may attempt things, but at the first sign of rejection and disappointment you quit.

- I'm not good enough.
- This is not for someone like me.
- They won't like me.

- I'm not special.

Are limiting beliefs holding you back? They can continually sabotage your relationships, your friendships, your marriage, even your sex life. They can negatively affect your relationships with your children. By perpetuating this cycle, you're affecting the risks you're willing to take, the adventures you're willing (or not) to have in pursuit of self-realisation and fulfilment. They can certainly have an impact on your work because they affect your confidence and make you doubt your ability, which can in turn affect your entire future. They can also have an impact on your health because beliefs control the entire body. These are all examples of the ways in which you can be limited by your belief system.

The belief 'I'm not' is a lie. Before we think or voice those words, we should remember that belief originally existed as someone else's opinion, and that person was likely conditioned by other people's opinions, which affected what they have said and done.

As stated earlier, you arrived as a clean canvas ready to be painted on, so all your beliefs were learned. Anything that is learned can be unlearned. You can reshape your beliefs to unlock the doors that have been holding you back, and claim your ultimate potential.

LIMITING BELIEFS

YOUR TIME IS NOW

"Question your beliefs to unlock the doors that are holding you back"
—MARIANA ARDELEAN

Change Your Beliefs

*Whatever the mind can conceive
and believe it can achieve.*
—Napoleon Hill

Whether your beliefs are holding you back from your next level of success, or are holding you back from your current level of success, you cannot grow beyond the belief system that you currently have. In other words, you must change your beliefs in order to change your life.

A perfect example of this is Roger Bannister. Before 1954, scientists and doctors believed it was impossible for a human being to run a mile in under four minutes. After carrying out all sorts of studies, they concluded that it was dangerous, and if anyone were to try it their heart might explode and their nervous system would overload, leading to certain death.

On 6th of May 1954, Roger Bannister was the first athlete to run a mile in less than four minutes because he didn't believe what the scientists and doctors believed. The most interesting part of this story is that, following Bannister's "death-defying" feat, many other athletes went on to run a mile in under four minutes, when only twelve months earlier no human being on the planet had even attempted it.

Research on the psychology of performance has found proven links between the mind and the body, and the conclusion is that both work in harmony. What you think and believe about yourself will manifest in your reality. Whether it happens now or later, the best thing you can do is unlock your potential so you can do what you never imagined you could do.

In order to take action you must follow a few simple steps. Whatever goal you have is the product of your habits, repeated over time, which is ignited by your behaviour, which is ignited by your choices, which are ignited by your beliefs.

You know you need to make a choice and you want to make that choice, but you don't do it. Why not? What stops you? Put simply, you're held back from making

CHANGE YOUR BELIEFS

the choice because of your beliefs. You only make choices that are in harmony with what you believe about yourself, your potential, and ultimately your future.

To change, you must have a goal, a desire, a reason. Why? Ask yourself what beliefs you need to uproot in order to accomplish your goals. What beliefs you need to hold onto in order to achieve your goals. Make the decision to draw a line in the sand and say: *This is it. I will not hold onto these beliefs any longer. I used to [insert belief here] but I'm getting better every day. I used to be overweight, but I'm getting thinner every day.* On a regular basis, immerse yourself with the new beliefs that you want to reinforce.

Another thing you can do is associate with people that you consider are better and smarter than you; studies have shown that we become the average of the five people we spend the most time with when it comes to attitude, health and income. As you choose to make changes in your life, associate with people who are focused on prosperity, health, or whatever else you're interested in. You might need to limit your association with people who are not helping you at the moment and instead associate with those who are.

Most of your beliefs exist on an unconscious level; you're not aware of them. Unless you become aware of your beliefs, and explore and question them, and then start to change those that are not serving you, they will hold you back.

You might sometimes feel that you're not making progress as quickly as you would like. By questioning your beliefs, you will open up new possibilities and opportunities that you didn't even know existed. In order to understand this, you must choose to have an open mind.

Most people usually operate on wish and hope: *I wish this would happen. I hope this will work. I hope I get it. I wish I could do that.* Unless you believe that you will achieve what you want, and you take action towards getting or doing those things, hoping and wishing alone will not get you there. You must do the thing that you're afraid of.

Courage is not the absence of fear. Courage is feeling the fear and taking action despite that fear. Whatever you fear, or whatever doubts you have about yourself, you must lean into those feelings and take a step forward. The only way to change your old patterns is to feel the fear and do it anyway. When you do, you will be on the cusp of an exciting journey.

Every time you feel something, act on it. If you want to achieve something, you must believe in it and take

CHANGE YOUR BELIEFS

action, even though you may not know exactly how to do that yet.

Your belief system is based on an evaluation of something: a thought, a situation, an experience. If you start questioning those beliefs and re-evaluate the specific situation or experience, your beliefs will change. Albert Einstein said, 'Not everything that counts can be counted and not everything that's counted truly counts.'

Believe that you can create a meaningful, fulfilling and purposeful life for yourself. Believe that you can make a difference and create meaning in someone else's life. Inside of you is your greater you. Sometimes all it takes is for someone to tell you that you're special, you're unique, you're worthy, you're capable; for someone to tell you that you can do this because they believe in you. They believe in you because someone believed in them when they didn't believe in themselves.

Most of us do the things we do to either gain pleasure or avoid pain. We are either moving towards pleasure or moving away from pain. Many people hold onto outdated beliefs that have been passed down through generations because those beliefs mean that they can avoid painful or uncomfortable emotions. Often, the uncomfortable emotion is fear. Fear of failure, fear of success, fear of not being good enough, fear of not belonging, fear of emotions, fear of change, and so on.

By understanding this, by slowly expanding your comfort zone and placing yourself in situations where you're uncertain of the outcome, or your skills, or whether you will be accepted, you will begin to confront your fear and slowly overcome that fear.

As you overcome your fear and expand your comfort zone, you will acquire a calmer attitude and the ability to face the emotional consequences of change. Accepting change will enable you to take calculated risks that you have possibly avoided in the past. You will expand the boundaries in your personal life as well as your professional life, and claim your ultimate potential.

On the other hand, if you cannot accept the change, you will likely remain where you are now, or perhaps find yourself in an even worse position. Where there is no growth, there is no progress.

Make a habit of doing one thing a day that is different from your normal way of doing things and slowly you will claim your ultimate potential. For instance, if you fear public speaking, you might benefit by joining an organisation like Toastmasters. It will give you the opportunity to practise speaking in an environment where you feel understood, and everyone else is there

CHANGE YOUR BELIEFS

for the same reason. By taking the necessary steps and putting yourself in this potentially uncomfortable situation, you will learn and grow, and slowly overcome the fear of public speaking. Plus, you will be proud of yourself for doing something that you were previously uncomfortable with.

If you're someone who likes to be in a position of control, you could consider becoming a volunteer at a homeless shelter, or perhaps volunteer at your local swimming pool. By doing this, you will be placed in a position where you have no choice but to let go of control. Instead, other people will be telling you what to do, and you will have to work cooperatively and possibly follow the instructions of others. Doing this may not make you feel comfortable, but you will have the opportunity to stretch, grow, and look at things from a different perspective.

It's important to believe in yourself and know yourself well, and, most importantly, believe that you can do it. If you believe you can, then you can.

Think about your current situation. What have you decided that you would like for yourself? You're about to do an exercise on beliefs, where you will write down the things that you feel are true for you. When you do this exercise, don't think too much about what to write.

YOUR TIME IS NOW

Just let your unconscious mind guide you and write what you feel. Write whatever comes to mind rather than overthinking it. You will gain more value from this exercise if you trust yourself.

Here are a few examples to get you started:

I always …
- do well at work.
- feel supported.
- like to make a difference.

I never …
- know what to do.
- like to doubt myself.
- like to be challenged.

I can't …
- change.
- try new things.
- be bothered.

I can …
- always learn anything I set my mind to.
- trust people.
- see the good in people.

CHANGE YOUR BELIEFS

I am
- full of life.
- funny.
- confident.
- always doubting myself.
- always worrying.
- always fearful.

Now think about this for moment and complete the following sentences:

I always

_____
_____
_____
_____
_____

I never

_____
_____
_____
_____

YOUR TIME IS NOW

I can't

I can

I am

CHANGE YOUR BELIEFS

What do I believe about myself?

_____
_____
_____
_____

What do I believe about my potential?

_____
_____
_____
_____

What do I believe about money?

_____
_____
_____
_____

YOUR TIME IS NOW

What do I believe about giving?

_____
_____
_____
_____
_____

What do I believe about studying?

_____
_____
_____
_____
_____

What do I believe about earning money?

_____
_____
_____
_____
_____

CHANGE YOUR BELIEFS

Do I believe money is easy or hard to earn?

_____
_____
_____
_____
_____

What is the purpose of my life?

_____
_____
_____
_____

What do relationships mean to me?

_____
_____
_____
_____
_____
_____

YOUR TIME IS NOW

What do I love?

_____
_____
_____
_____
_____

What am I passionate about?

_____
_____
_____
_____
_____

Who would I like to be? What would it take for me to become that person?

_____
_____
_____
_____
_____
_____

CHANGE YOUR BELIEFS

What do I value in my life?

_____
_____
_____
_____
_____

What are my expectations of life?

_____
_____
_____
_____
_____

What am I avoiding in my life?

_____
_____
_____
_____
_____
_____

YOUR TIME IS NOW

What drives me mad?

_____
_____
_____
_____
_____

When do I feel love?

_____
_____
_____
_____
_____

When do I feel safe?

_____
_____
_____
_____
_____

CHANGE YOUR BELIEFS

How do I meet my need for adventure?

_____
_____
_____
_____
_____

When do I feel special and unique?

_____
_____
_____
_____
_____

When do I feel loved?

_____
_____
_____
_____
_____

YOUR TIME IS NOW

What has to happen for me to feel angry?

_____
_____
_____
_____
_____

What has to happen for me to feel sad?

_____
_____
_____
_____
_____

In what way do I believe my thoughts could be getting in my way?

_____
_____
_____
_____
_____

CHANGE YOUR BELIEFS

In what ways do I have unrealistic expectations of myself?

_____
_____
_____
_____
_____

In what ways am I too hard on myself?

_____
_____
_____
_____
_____

What do I feel I always have to do?

_____
_____
_____
_____
_____

YOUR TIME IS NOW

Where in my body do I feel stuck or held back?

_____
_____
_____
_____
_____

What do I think that feeling might be trying to protect me from?

_____
_____
_____
_____
_____

What holds me back?

_____
_____
_____
_____
_____

CHANGE YOUR BELIEFS

How do I stand in my own way?

_____
_____
_____
_____
_____

What do I avoid? How does this avoidance affect my life?

_____
_____
_____
_____
_____

What do I avoid feeling? How does this impact me in my life?

_____
_____
_____
_____
_____

YOUR TIME IS NOW

What would be the worst insult someone could throw at me?

What's getting in the way here?

What would make me feel silly to say out loud?

CHANGE YOUR BELIEFS

What rules do I have about how I should behave that are getting in the way of me moving forward?

_____
_____
_____
_____
_____

What is it that I believe that keeps me from being fully myself?

_____
_____
_____
_____
_____

After answering these questions, ask yourself if your beliefs serve you, support you, nurture you or challenge you. Just because you don't know exactly how to do something, that doesn't mean that you can't do it. By changing your beliefs, you're changing what you're capable of, and putting yourself in control of what you want to accomplish in your life to claim your ultimate potential.

If you think it's hard to earn money, it *will* be hard to earn money. With that belief, you will look for ways of earning money the hard way. If you think something is difficult, you will find reasons to justify your belief in that difficulty. The only thing you will see is what you believe, what you focus on, the things you are in harmony with, what's actually going on inside you. You will filter out the rest, even if you're not aware that you're doing it. As the saying goes, 'As you believe, so is it done unto you.'

You can change your beliefs through spaced repetition, and your new beliefs will become integrated with who you truly are.

Another method is to use a significant event in your life, like a major accident, the death of a love one, or finding out that you have cancer. Most people have around seven significant events in their lives. Rather than waiting for a significant event to happen in your life, you can choose to use space repetition to make the changes that you truly want.

Over the years, especially in the field of personal development, the method of spaced repetition has been shown to work well. Simply put, what this means is that

CHANGE YOUR BELIEFS

once you know your newfound beliefs, every day you read them out loud first thing in the morning and then again in the evening just before you go to bed. Do this until they have become integrated with who you want to become.

Most people have around seven significant events in their lives. The moment a significant event happens they make a committed decision to change, and they do so without hesitation.

If you believe in yourself and your abilities, and in others, then others will believe in you.

Some examples of beliefs that I use and that work for me:

- All I need is within me now.
- I do what I say and say what I mean.
- I am great at trying new things.
- If I learn, then I will earn.
- I am willing to learn how to succeed.
- I will find a way.
- People are amazing.
- Consistency is the key to success.
- Persistency pays.

YOUR TIME IS NOW

If you uncover some beliefs that you may feel are not in alignment with who you want to be, what can you do to change them?

Your new belief:

_____
_____
_____
_____
_____
_____
_____
_____
_____
_____
_____
_____
_____
_____
_____
_____
_____
_____
_____
_____

CHANGE YOUR BELIEFS

YOUR TIME IS NOW

Once you have written down your new beliefs, you can consciously decide to make time to focus on them. This could be in the morning when you wake up, or in the evening before you go to bed. Read them aloud to yourself. If you do this on a regular basis, your subconscious mind will start looking for evidence that supports the beliefs you're reading aloud. In time you will form new neuropathways, because neurones that fire together, wire together.

Attitude

Everything can be taken from a man but one thing: the last of the human freedoms— to choose one's attitude in any given set of circumstances, to choose one's own way.
—Victor E Frankl

Brian Tracy said, 'Your attitude is an expression of your values, beliefs, and expectations.' Your attitude is the way you express your values and beliefs, through either your behaviour or the words you choose to describe them.

Attitude is made up of three components:

- Cognition: Your thoughts and beliefs about something or someone

YOUR TIME IS NOW

- Emotions: How a person, object, issues, or an event makes you feel
- Behaviour: How your attitude influences your behaviour

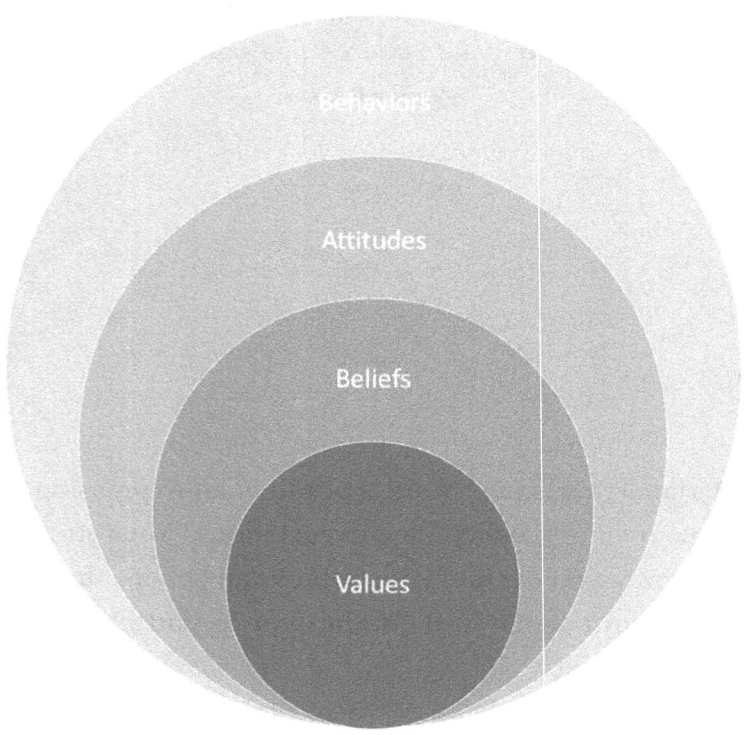

It's your actions and feelings that determine what you do and how you feel about yourself and others. Your attitude determines and shapes your everyday actions, and your everyday actions determine your results. Some people's ideas and actions will culminate in extraordinary achievements while other people's ideas and actions will be marked by repeated frustration, the feeling of being overwhelmed, and problems in their lives. They may not even realise that this is because of their attitude.

Your attitude is something you have control over. Whether you realise this or not, your attitude tells others how you feel, and what your expectations are. Everyone you come in contact with will reflect your attitude back to you. If you're happy and smile, and have the expectation of happiness in your life, others will reflect happiness and cheerfulness back to you. When you're happy and share this happiness openly, others will be attracted to you.

In other words, you get back what you put out. By understanding this principle, and knowing that your attitude determines the quality of your life, you will soon realise that you have a choice: you can choose to change the way you look at things, the way you approach things, and the way you deal with any situation that arises.

Your attitude is the most important component you need to live a fulfilled life and to claim your ultimate potential. Your surroundings also reflect who you are; in other words, your environment is the mirror of you. As soon as you show a willingness to change, and actually start to change, your surroundings and your environment will change as well.

If you have a great attitude, you will end up with great results. If you have an average attitude, you will end up with average results. And if you have a poor attitude, you will end up with poor results.

The quality of your life and the way you live are both determined by your beliefs, values, attitude and behaviour. When you understand that your results are determined by your attitude, you can begin the process of changing your life for the better.

You might think it all seems quite simple, but it's not as easy as it sounds. Learning new habits and changing attitudes takes time. Like anything, changing your habits and your attitude requires determination, discipline, perseverance, consistency, and, most importantly, making the decision and being willing to change. Studies have shown that it takes on average sixty-six days to change a habit, which is why most people give up before

ATTITUDE

a new habit has become engrained in their unconscious mind.

The majority of people never consider how their attitude or behaviour impacts their everyday lives. They react without taking responsibility or thinking about the situation. In my time as a health professional, I have come across this daily, especially with patients who end up waiting longer than their expected waiting times. People deal with this situation in two very different ways. Some are happy, calm and content, even when they have to wait longer than anticipated. While others complain and question the situation. They ask why it's taking so long or why other people are being attended to before them. They don't stop to consider that every person is there for a different reason and that some appointments take longer depending on the specific needs of the patient.

Having a great attitude is important because your attitude is what determines your level of fulfilment, happiness, satisfaction—and your results. It also allows you to claim your ultimate potential. Someone with an attitude of failure, for example, will be doomed before they even begin. It's likely that they won't even attempt to start something because they already believe they will fail.

YOUR TIME IS NOW

William James, the father of psychology, said, 'Human beings can alter their lives by altering their attitude of mind.' If we think about this, someone with a bad attitude will perhaps at some point find themselves in unpleasant, difficult circumstances. When they experience a difficult situation in their life, it's because of their attitude. By reacting to the circumstances, they will reinforce the bad attitude, hence bringing even more drama into their life. As they say, 'We get what we expect.'

Many people have difficulty with the thought that their life, and the way they experience the world around them, is a reflection of their attitude. Their attitude may be that if someone smiles at them they will smile at that person in return. They don't consider that if they smile first, the other person will smile back at them.

Another good analogy refers to the person who sits in front of the fireplace waiting to warm up without putting any wood onto or lighting the fire. Without the spark, there can be no fire. Without fire, there can be no heat. They have to act first, and the consequences will follow. Every action and inaction has its own set of consequences.

There are steps you can take if you choose to improve your attitude. Start by being grateful and acknowledging

ATTITUDE

yourself for where you are. Wake up with a sense of gratitude every morning, and you'll find that your life will begin to change.

Your attitude is a reflection of the person you are. Someone might be successful at what they do, but that does not mean they won't sometimes fail. Those with the right attitude will be able to move forward. They will ask themselves what they can learn from their failure, how they can improve, and what they can do better next time. The crucial thing to remember is this: they keep going. That's an outstanding attitude to have and the reason successful people get exceptional results.

People who achieve exceptional results usually have a matching attitude. They have the attitude that they can accomplish things. They have the attitude that they are competent. They have the attitude of expectancy. And because of that attitude they achieve exceptional results as they claim their ultimate potential.

Frequently, these people are no more talented or smarter than the average person; they simply have the right attitude. They believe in themselves and take actions that help move them forward, closer towards their desired dreams.

The way you look at things, and the way you do things—in other words, your attitude—will make you come alive, and you will attract people who will seek you out, who will want to help you and want to spend quality time with you.

Think of your environment—the world in which you live, where you work, your relationships—as a mirror of your attitude. Once you feel, think and see that your environment can do with some improvement, you can turn things around simply by improving your attitude. After all, your attitude doesn't affect other people as much as it affects you.

Most people fail to understand that nothing will change unless *they* change and that when they change their perception, the whole world will change with them. This is all about attitude. Many relationships and marriages fall apart because one person feels that their partner needs to change, in some way, without considering that perhaps they are the one who needs to change their behaviour or attitude.

By having a can-do or will-do attitude, you will begin to see things from a different perspective, even during the tough times. As Thomas Jefferson said, 'Nothing can stop the man with the right mental attitude from achieving his goal, nothing on earth can help the man with the wrong mental attitude.'

ATTITUDE

Developing your attitude

So, how do you develop the right attitude? First, you must be aware that you *need* to develop the right attitude. That's the first step towards acquiring the right attitude. Start by reminding yourself of this every morning. Put a Post-it note next to your bed, or on the bathroom mirror. Put another one in your car, and another at work. Or use technology and send yourself reminders on your phone, or email yourself with the note: *Smile!*

Start by saying hello to people. Make sure you're kind and loving towards yourself first, and then towards others. Once you begin to develop, and then maintain, an attitude that says yes—yes to you, yes to life, and yes to everything around you—you will be amazed at all the changes you suddenly start to notice taking place in your life.

When you start believing in yourself and change your attitude, you will act like the person you want to become, and that will become your new reality. Goethe, the great German poet, philosopher and literary figure, said, 'Before you can do something, you must first be something.'

And now it's time to do another exercise. After you've done this exercise, you should feel better, and perhaps you will inspire someone else to feel better, too. This will change your attitude because you will be adding meaning to your own life as well as to someone else's.

Starting from tomorrow, smile at every person you encounter. Acknowledge them by saying hello. You will discover that it's possible to make a difference in someone else's life simply by smiling at them, and you will feel better yourself. This simple yet very powerful exercise has the ability to change the way you feel, see and think. By making eye contact with the person you smile at, you're changing your physiology, and when you change your physiology you will also begin to change your psychology.

Every day, adopt the attitude that says you're a successful person. Treat everyone you come into contact with as though they are important and successful. By doing this on a regular basis, eventually it will become a habit.

If someone is rude to you, you can choose to react or you can choose to smile—it's up to you. By choosing to smile, you will feel different. You will feel in control of the situation and that will enable you to hold onto your power. If someone cuts you off in traffic, instead of getting upset, frustrated or angry, choose to smile instead. It's your choice.

ATTITUDE

Emotions such as frustration, anger, jealousy and betrayal, and any other emotions that surface when you're upset with someone, will only hurt *you*, not others, because *you*'re the one feeling those emotions. Being aware of this and understanding it is very important because it can impact all areas of your life in the long term. Also, holding onto things that have happened in the past, things that you may not necessarily have agreed with, will not serve you, either. Forgive yourself first and then forgive others. Let things go. Let the past stay in the past, and you will feel better.

As you develop your new attitude, know that you're placing yourself in the top five percent of people. Your fulfilment in life will depend on how well you're able to relate to others. Other people's attitudes towards you will also depend on your attitude towards them. By developing your attitude, you will claim your ultimate potential.

> *Surround yourself with the dreamers and doers, the believers and thinkers, but most of all, surround yourself with those who see the greatest within you, even when you don't see it yourself.*
> —Edmund Lee

YOUR TIME IS NOW

Ask yourself the following questions regarding your attitude:

What is my attitude towards myself?

_____
_____
_____
_____
_____
_____
_____
_____
_____
_____
_____
_____
_____
_____
_____
_____
_____

ATTITUDE

YOUR TIME IS NOW

What is my attitude towards others?

_____
_____
_____
_____
_____

What is my attitude towards my job?

_____
_____
_____
_____
_____

What is my attitude towards life?

_____
_____
_____
_____
_____
_____

ATTITUDE

What is my attitude towards my family?

_____
_____
_____
_____

What is my attitude towards my children?

_____
_____
_____
_____

What is my attitude towards my partner?

_____
_____
_____
_____
_____

YOUR TIME IS NOW

What is my attitude towards my colleagues?

_____
_____
_____
_____
_____

What is my attitude in general?

_____
_____
_____
_____
_____

What is my attitude towards my boss?

_____
_____
_____
_____
_____

ATTITUDE

"A large part of our attitude towards things is conditioned by opinions and emotions which we unconsciously absorb as children from our environment. In other words, it is tradition—besides inherited aptitudes and qualities—which makes us what we are. We but rarely reflect how relatively small as compared with the powerful influence of tradition is the influence of our conscious thought upon our conduct and convictions."

—Albert Einstein

YOUR TIME IS NOW

"The quality of your life and the way you live are both determined by your beliefs, values, attitude and behaviour"
—Mariana Ardelean

Standards

> *Let us be about setting high standards for life, love, creativity, and wisdom. If our expectations in these areas are low, we are not likely to experience wellness. Setting high standards makes every day and every decade worth looking forward to.*
>
> **—Greg Anderson**

According to Tony Robbins, 'When you have high expectations of yourself that's when you raise your standards.' Your standards are the only thing that will create change in your life. So if you want to change your life, you must raise your standards. When you raise your standards, you change your behaviour. When you change your behaviour, you change your habits. When you change your habits, you start to create different practices. When you carry out different practices on a regular basis, you will find a way to achieve your desired results and claim your ultimate potential.

You base your standards on your environment and with whom you spend time with. Jim Rohn said, 'You are the average of the five people you spend the most time with.' And who you spend time with is who you become.

Author and businessman T. Harv Eker highlights the significance of standards. In his book, *Secrets of the Millionaire Mind*, he states, 'How you do anything is how you do everything.' If you consider one single incident, you could end up being more tolerant of yourself, and what you thought was just a one-off exception will become the standard for you. If you drop your standards, your ability to claim your ultimate potential and achieve your goals will drop as well.

It's important to realise that a single event in any given situation doesn't matter. What does matter is how you respond to that event when you come across it on a regular basis, and the standards you uphold for yourself. Your ability to create success and fulfilment in your life is determined by your standards. Do you do what you say you're going to do? Are you keeping your promises

STANDARDS

to yourself? Are you upholding your commitments to others?

When I talk about standards, both personal or business, I'm talking about what you believe is and is not acceptable, and what you believe is okay and is not okay in your mind.

When it comes to doing something, do you find it challenging or easy? Do you think you can only focus on something for a couple of hours, or do you think you will do whatever it takes to achieve the outcome that you want? Your standards determine your results.

If you're late getting to work or an appointment, even if it's only by a couple of minutes, that's a poor standard, because if you let one thing slip, you will let other things slip. From a psychological point, if you let yourself down, you're likely to let others down as well. Understanding and knowing this is important. How you do anything is how you do everything. Your behaviours are built on the expectations you have for yourself and others.

Your standards are reflected in the way you treat yourself and others, as well as how you expect to be treated yourself. If you have high standards, you expect to be held in high regard. If you have low standards, you tolerate things as they are, and allow people to walk all over you. Not standing up for yourself is also an indication of low self-esteem. Holding yourself accountable, and taking personal responsibility for your standards is crucial, especially if you want to create change in your life and raise your self-esteem.

Your standards are also reflected in the promises you keep, in the way you present yourself, and how you look after yourself, your finances, your life and the environment around you. Are you organised or disorganised at home and at work? This is a reflection of the standards you uphold in these areas of your life.

Your standards are reflected in the quality of your work, your ability to communicate, the things you value, and what you believe. In fact, everything you say and do provides others with specific insights into the standards you hold yourself to. Therefore you may need to embrace discipline when it comes to the quality of the work you produce, and the environment around you. You could start to exercise and eat healthier meals instead of junk food. You could watch your spending habits, especially if you intend to build wealth.

Regardless of whether you're aware of this or not, you're always letting others know how you feel about any circumstance in your life, how you feel about yourself, and how you feel about others. At the same time, you're

STANDARDS

being judged by others based on the messages you're sending.

When it comes down to achieving your goals in any area of your life, your standards will determine the outcome. If you have low standards, you will likely struggle to invest the time, effort and energy that is required to achieve your intended results. If you have high standards, it is likely you will have different expectations of what is possible, what you're prepared to do, and what actions you will take. You will also have a different view of what you expect from others.

When you raise your standards, your expectations will also be raised, and you will be more prepared and willing to put in the time and effort to get results. In doing this, you will attract more opportunities and possibilities into your life because you will be acting with confidence.

The majority of people fail to achieve the desired results they crave in their lives because they have low standards and expectations. These low standards lead to average results.

Remember, the quality of your results will determine the quality of your life. If you want the results and the quality of your life to change, it's essential to understand that *you* must change first. Otherwise, nothing else will change. If you reach a point in your life where you're tired of your current circumstances and feel that you've had enough, acknowledge that nothing will change unless *you* do. Then you can make the decision to turn things around.

> *Hold yourself responsible for a higher standard than anybody else expects of you.*
> —**Henry Ward Beecher**

Consider your current behaviour, reality, actions and results, and ask yourself the following questions:

What standards do I currently have?

_____
_____
_____
_____
_____
_____
_____
_____
_____
_____

STANDARDS

What standards do I have for myself in different circumstances?

_____
_____
_____
_____
_____

What is my behaviour like in those circumstances?

_____
_____
_____
_____
_____

What actions do I take in those circumstances?

_____
_____
_____
_____
_____

YOUR TIME IS NOW

What standards do I have as a parent?

___

What standards do I have as a friend?

___

What standards do I have as a sister/brother?

___

STANDARDS

What standards do I have as a professional?

_____
_____
_____
_____
_____

What will I accept for myself?

_____
_____
_____
_____
_____

What will I no longer accept for myself?

_____
_____
_____
_____
_____
_____

YOUR TIME IS NOW

What expectations do I have of myself?

_____
_____
_____
_____
_____

What expectations do I have of others?

_____
_____
_____
_____
_____

What practices do I currently have?

_____
_____
_____
_____
_____

STANDARDS

What practices am I willing to implement?

_____
_____
_____
_____

Are my standards truly mine?

_____
_____
_____
_____

Did I set my standards for myself?

_____
_____
_____
_____
_____

YOUR TIME IS NOW

If I didn't set my own standards, who did, and when?

_____
_____
_____
_____
_____

Why did I adopt my current standards?

_____
_____
_____
_____
_____

Given the expected results, are my standards preventing me in any way?

_____
_____
_____
_____
_____

STANDARDS

Examples of standards:

- I take full responsibility for my actions and results.
- I keep promises to myself and others.
- I do what I say and say what I do.
- I stay true to my values.
- I respect myself and everyone I meet.
- I exercise three to five times a week.

Your standards

YOUR TIME IS NOW

Success Practices

*You'll never change your life until you
change something you do daily. The secret of
your success is found in your daily routine.*

—JOHN C MAXWELL

If you're after a fulfilling, prosperous, satisfying and happy life, you could consider introducing a morning and evening practice into your life. Many successful people—multimillionaires, top managers, CEOs and TV personalities—are early risers and typically achieve a lot before the rest of the population has even considered waking up.

A morning and evening practice is not just about waking up early and going to bed at a specific time. It's as much about what you *want* as what you *do*. If you change the way you think, along with your daily habits, you can achieve your desired results and claim your ultimate potential.

By having specific practices, you will discover what it takes for you to reach your goals, why hitting the snooze button is costing you more than you actually think, and how to follow through with healthy habits. For example, you might think it's okay to skip your morning routine since you can always do it the following day. But that decision does not just affect that moment in time, it also affects the person you're becoming.

As mentioned in the previous chapter, author and businessman T Harv Eker highlighted the significance of this habit when he wrote: 'How you do anything is how you do everything.' If you consider a single event you may end up being more tolerant of yourself, and the event you were thinking of as a one-off exception will become the standard for you. As you drop your standards, your ability to claim your ultimate potential and your goals will decrease as well.

If you have the desire to create and live life on your terms, you must consider changing the way you think, and how you do things on a regular basis. Dwelling on the past and making excuses will only delay your success and your desired outcome. Jim Rohn said, 'If you want

SUCCESS PRACTICES

to have more, you have to become more. For things to change, you have to change. For things to get better, you have to get better. For things to improve, you have to improve. If you grow, everything grows for you.'

According to the neuroscientist, Antonio Damasio, when it comes to decision-making, though most of us believe that we use logic to make decisions, it is actually our feelings that decide for us 95 percent of the time. This is because we are a 'feeling machine that thinks' not a 'thinking machine that feels'.

In his research, Damasio studied people who had brain damage and were unable to experience any emotions. He discovered that the subjects were unable to make decisions. They could logically describe what they thought they should do, and were aware of each of the pros and cons, but ultimately, they could not decide on what to do. This happened with even the simplest of choices, like deciding what to eat.

When you ask yourself the question, 'What do I want to eat?' what you're actually asking yourself is, 'What do I feel like eating?' Whenever you ask yourself a question that relates to the act of doing something, you're actually checking in with your feelings and basing your decision on them. If it's something you haven't done before, something that's daunting or challenging, you may hesitate because your feelings are clouding your judgements.

Most of the time, your feelings are not aligned with what you want. If you feel uncertain, insecure, or that you think you will be judged or rejected, you may never take a chance on doing the thing that you want or would love to do.

If you only make decisions when you feel certain, secure, or externally validated by others, you will never achieve your desired goals and dreams. Having the ability to separate your feelings from the actions you need to take, and at the right time, is essential for your success at claiming your ultimate potential.

When you don't feel like doing something: push yourself. Could you take the necessary steps to do it? Put yourself out there. If you can do that, you will move forward, and you will achieve your desired results. You just need to have the ability to untangle your feeling from your actions; otherwise, you will never unlock your true potential. Especially with something that is important and does need your consideration, you might find that you talk yourself out of doing it, and you struggle to stick to your promises. Even though you want to do it, you can't stick to anything that's uncomfortable because you're battling with your feelings. This happens even

SUCCESS PRACTICES

though you know that you're more than capable of doing the work—and of change—regardless of how you feel.

You may not be able to control your emotions, but you can consciously choose how to behave in any given situation. Decide to act on the facts instead of acting on emotions or feelings. Sometimes you will need to ignore your feelings in order to achieve the outcome you want.

By taking action, your confidence and self-esteem will improve. Social psychologist, Timothy Wilson, whose field is psychological intervention, wrote: 'Do good, be good.' This principle dates back to Aristotle.

By changing your behaviour first, you will improve your perception of the kind of person that you are and the things you can do. Being able to push through the feelings that stop you, being able to do the work to break the habits that hold you back, and being able to replace those habits, with better habits, will enable you to move forward in the direction you really desire to go.

To be able to pursue what's truly important to you, you must act with courage and confidence in the face of doubts, and prove to yourself that you're capable of being more. Then you will *do* more, and in turn have the satisfaction of knowing that you can accomplish whatever you set out to do.

YOUR TIME IS NOW

So, are you convinced that you want to change your life? Are you asking where you should begin? This may be the answer you're looking for. Start by employing just a few basic techniques that will give you inspiration every single evening and morning, starting with sleep.

Sleep

> *Sleep is that golden chain that ties health and our bodies together.*
> —Thomas Dekker

By employing just a few basic techniques in your life, starting with your sleeping habits, you will gain the inspiration to change. Sleep is a necessary part of life, yet many of us, including me, ignore the consequences of getting by with as little sleep as possible, or oversleeping on weekends. Making a few adjustments to the way you think about sleep, starting with the time you go to bed, will have a significant impact on your quality of life, and the way you see and do things as you claim your ultimate potential. You can make significant differences to your life simply by following your biological clock, also known as the circadian system, which is a twenty-four-hour cycle. In his book, *The Power of When*, Dr Michael Breus writes: 'There is a perfect time to do just about anything.' This includes sleep, according to your chronotype and your circadian rhythms.

By making tiny adjustments to your daily practice—starting with when to go to bed, when to wake up, when to exercise, when to have sex, when to eat, when to drink coffee, when to have an alcoholic drink, when to have a shower or bath, when to learn something new—you can synchronise the rhythm of your day with your circadian rhythm. Then everything will start to feel natural and at ease.

Even if you don't change what you do or how you do it, and you only make changes to *when* you do it, you will be healthier and a lot more resourceful.

Your inner, or biological, clock is regulated by a group of nerves called suprachiasmatic nucleus (SCN), located right above the pituitary gland in the hypothalamus in the brain, which is considered the master of the hormonal system. In the morning, when sunlight reaches your eyes and travels down through the optic nerves, your SCN is activating to begin your circadian rhythm and signals to you that it is time to wake up. The SCN is the master clock that controls other clocks in the body.

SLEEP

Your inner clock controls and commands your sleep, core temperature, appetite, blood pressure, hormones, energy, fatigue, metabolism, alertness, creativity, healing ability and many other functions. All this is happening whether you realise it or not.

For thousands of years, our hunter-gatherer ancestors scheduled their daily practice according to their inner clock, rising at sunlight, spending most of the day outdoors, and going to sleep at nightfall. As we advanced as a species—especially after electricity and the incandescent light bulb were introduced by Thomas Edison on 31 December 1879—our inner clocks started to be disrupted. We no longer wake up at dawn and go to sleep at nightfall. Most of us no longer work from dawn to dusk or go to sleep at nightfall. We no longer spend our time outdoors in the sun, working from dawn until dusk, to come home to our last meal at twilight.

These days we do shift work, and spend a lot of time indoors, where, a great deal of the time, we are exposed to artificial light. With advances in technology, we are now connected to digital devices 24/7, and because of this our inner clocks are out of balance.

We also now have the ability to travel through multiple time zones within hours instead of days, which leaves us with jet lag and out of sync with our inner clocks. When I travel overseas, especially to Europe, I notice that it takes less time to adjust when I arrive compared to when I return to Australia. Last time it took me nearly a week to recover from my jet lag.

Being out of sync affects us emotionally, mentally and physically. This is known as chrono-misalignment, and is implicated in obesity, cancer, heart disease, diabetes and mood disorders. Symptoms can include insomnia, with the resulting sleep deprivation leading, in some cases, to anxiety, depression, frustration, a feeling of being overwhelmed, weight gain, stress, and poor performance.

Every single one of us has a biological clock, but not every biological clock runs on the same bio-time because some people are early risers and some are late risers. According to past wisdom, there are three chronotypes: larks, who are early risers; owls, who are late risers; and hummingbirds, who are neither late nor early risers. About ten percent of the population are excluded from these three categories, and also don't match individual personality profiles. Because of this, Dr Michael Breus has redefined people into four chronotypes. The groups are named for mammals rather than birds: dolphins, lions, bears and wolves.

SLEEP

Dolphins are light sleepers and account for ten percent of the population. Lions are early risers and account for 15–20 percent of the population. Bears, who wake and sleep according to the rise and fall of the sun, account for 50 percent of the population. Wolves are late risers, and account for 15–20 percent of the population.

If you would like to take a bio-time quiz to find out your chronotype, go to the website thepowerofwhen.com. If you would like more details about when is the best time to do anything, I highly recommend the book, *The Power of When*.

Depending on your chronotype, to get enough good-quality sleep you must have at least four, preferably five, sleep cycles each night. Each sleep cycle lasts for about ninety minutes.

The first couple of sleep cycles are known as delta sleep, which is deep sleep, the part of sleep where the body builds up energy for the following day. This is when the body stimulates growth and development, and repairs bones and muscle. It's also when the immune system is boosted. Deep sleep is essential for our health, and for us to feel energised and refreshed the following day.

The last two to three cycles are when we experience lighter sleep, when we consolidate our dreams and our memories. This is when rapid eye movement (REM) takes place.

Sometimes, even after a full night's sleep, you might wake up feeling groggy because your alarm was set to go off in the middle of a sleep cycle. To work out the optimum bedtime for you, take into consideration your normal wake time during the week and then work backwards. Keep in mind that it takes 20–40 minutes to doze off.

According to Dr Michael Breus, lions and bears should calculate seven and a half hours' sleep: 90 minutes x 5 cycles = 450 minutes + another 20 minutes to fall asleep, totalling 470 minutes.

Dolphins should calculate 90 minutes x 4 cycles = 360 minutes + another 40 minutes to fall asleep, totalling 400 minutes.

Wolves should calculate 90 minutes x 4 cycles = 360 minutes + another 40 minutes to fall asleep + another 20 minutes of semiconscious rest REM between the alarm going off and actually getting out of bed, totalling 420 minutes.

To summarise:

- Lions: wake-up time 5.00 am; 470 minutes of sleep: bedtime 9.10 pm

SLEEP

- Bears: wake-up time 7.00 am; 470 minutes of sleep: bedtime 11.10 pm
- Dolphins: wake-up time 6.30 am; 400 minutes of sleep: bedtime 11.50 pm
- Wolves: wake-up time 7.00am; 420 minutes of sleep: bedtime 12.00 am (midnight)

Use this formula and, working backwards, start to implement it into your evening practice as you claim your ultimate potential. This will only work if you *make* it work, and if you choose to apply and comply with the principles. Even though most of us know what to do, we often fail to follow through with it.

Research shows us that most people delay sleep at least a couple of times a week. When it comes to going to bed on time, procrastination is a choice that we make, even though we know we'll feel awful in the morning. Just like choosing to eat junk food instead of fruit and vegetables; we know it's not good for us, but we still do it anyway.

To increase your chances of going to bed on time, it's imperative that you have an evening practice, starting with reducing the amount of time you spend in front of electronic devices that emit blue light. This includes tablets, computers, smartphones, and even the TV. Turn off all of your devices at least ninety minutes before going to bed. This will allow your levels of melatonin and cortisol to normalise.

Another way of reducing the effects of blue light, while still being able to use your devices, is to invest in a pair of Swannies Classic glasses. They have anti-reflective and anti-glare coating on the lenses, which protect your eyes from the blue light and lessen eyestrain.

Your evening practice can vary, depending on your choices: prepare for the next day; follow a hygiene routine by taking off makeup, brushing your teeth and having a shower or bath; have a relaxing conversation with a loved one; read a book or magazine; keep a journal acknowledging yourself and noting your gratitude for the day; read books that help you connect with your values, beliefs, standards, affirmations, goals; meditate.

Set your intention for the next day and enjoy your beauty sleep. Before you know it, your alarm will sound and you will be tempted to press the snooze button.

Snooze Button

> *There is too much life to be loved for you to hit the snooze button. In fact, I believe it is "seize the day", not "snooze the day"!*
> —**Hal Elrod**

To start the day well, you must stop hitting the snooze button and find out more about sleep. Did you hit the snooze button this morning? Many people are guilty of this. So, what's the problem? Well, hitting the snooze button keeps you from waking up with a sense of purpose. Each time you hit the button, you're subconsciously saying to yourself that you don't want to wake up to your experiences, and that you're not looking forward to the day ahead.

YOUR TIME IS NOW

When you want to change anything, it's up to you. It's your decision, and if you're going to change anything, you need to act differently despite your feelings. Once you master one area of your life, you will be able to master any other area of your life that you choose to improve.

At any time you want to change anything in your life and you will feel resistance, if you learn to lean in and work through that resistance, you will feel the inner strength to get things done. You will be able to set yourself up and put yourself in a better position, which means you won't be tempted to push the snooze button.

Before heading to bed, set the intention that you'll rise the next morning feeling invigorated. If you can persuade yourself to look forward to the next day, for whatever reason, waking up will be a lot easier. After you've set your intention, move your alarm away from your bed. Make sure you have to physically get out of bed to turn it off. And once you're out of bed, make the conscious decision not to get back in again.

When you wake up without pressing the snooze button, you will automatically feel a sense of satisfaction because you have taken the first step in taking control of your life.

SNOOZE BUTTON

When you finally understand that your feelings influence and dictate your actions, then you can stop thinking about how you feel and instead focus on what's important to you, and what you need to do in order to become the person you want to be

By keeping promises to yourself, your confidence in yourself will increase, and you will be able to take this strength into any other area of your life. When you make the decision to start something, you're being courageous. And if you stick with that decision, that takes further courage. And if you share what you're doing with others, then you're being even more courageous.

By building discipline and having a daily morning practice, you will be able to bridge the gap between the person you're now and the person you want to become, even though it may feel impossible at times. By taking the first step, you're building that bridge, you're closing that gap, and that's what's important. It takes courage to say yes to yourself.

Sometimes the first step is the hardest. You will have days when you won't feel like it. I know I did. I had days when I didn't feel like waking up, or didn't wake up in time. Taking the first step is important, because you have the ability to get back on track any time you fall off the wagon. What it comes down to is that you don't have to *feel* like it, you just have to *do* it. Do it for yourself and stay on the path. Building a new practice (habit) may not be easy, but if you persist it will be worth it.

By making the decision to have a morning and evening practice, you're taking control of your life, one day at a time. The choice that you make will be a game changer for your life, and the lives of the people around you. By setting your intention for the day, you're influencing other areas of your life.

Now let's come back to the snooze button.

You should never press the snooze button. Why? Because researchers have shown the negative neurological effects of doing this. Hitting the snooze button has a negative impact on the brain's function, as well as productivity, and those effects can last for up to four hours.

Also, it's important to remember that you sleep in 90-minute cycles. About two hours before you wake up, your body starts to prepare itself to wake up *slowly*, so that when the alarm goes off your body is already in wake-up mode.

When you hit the snooze button, your body drifts back to sleep, forcing your brain to start a new 90-minute sleep cycle. When the alarm goes off again after eight

SNOOZE BUTTON

minutes, however, the cortical region of your brain—the part of the brain responsible for decision-making, alertness and self-control—is still in this sleep cycle. This portion of the brain won't be able to wake up for another eighty-two minutes because it needs to finish what the snooze button started. If you do this, it can take anywhere from two to four hours for the additional sleep-cycle effects to wear off and for all your cognitive functions to return to full capacity.

If you press the snooze button a few times, you're starting a new sleep cycle each time, which will then be interrupted. When you eventually do wake up, you won't feel very well; you'll feel as though you didn't get enough sleep.

Knowing this now, what are you going to do from now on? Are you going to press the snooze button or are you going to get up?

By moving your alarm out of reach, you won't be tempted to turn it off and go back to sleep. Once you're out of bed and have switched off the alarm, head straight to the bathroom, wash your face and brush your teeth. Doing this will give you a feeling of freshness; you will feel more awake and ready for the day ahead.

For those people who suffer from depression, the morning is often the hardest time of the day. But anyone who struggles to wake up in the morning reduces their chances of enjoying a satisfying day ahead.

I'm guilty of hitting the snooze button myself, and did so on a regular basis for years, before I knew what I know now. I sometimes hit the button two, three or even four times, and arrived late to work, thinking it was okay because my receptionist was always there on time, opening up and turning everything on for me. I did this for years. I was stuck in what researchers call a 'habit loop'. But being down and depressed wasn't working for me, so I had to pay attention and start doing things differently. The moment I decided to change and look at things from a different perspective, everything changed.

I carried around Tony Robbins' program, 'Unleash the Power Within', for more than nine years before I looked at it. Then one day I decided to listen to it in the car. It was a decision that changed my life, as I've realised that nothing will change unless I do.

Having a daily practice helped me prioritise the day ahead. I felt more in control, and was clearer about what to focus on and what was important on a daily basis. I started to see opportunities that I didn't know existed.

You can create any morning practice that you like, whatever suits you. Most successful people have had great success in adding exercise, meditation and reading to their morning practice. Experiment and see what works for you. You can stick with that, or change it from time to time.

Take a look at Oprah Winfrey, Bill Gates, Albert Einstein and even Aristotle, and ask yourself what they have in common. They all had the same practice in the morning: they got up early.

If you find it challenging to wake up in the morning, try changing the way you think about sleep. Ask yourself if you've ever woken up completely exhausted on a special day. Probably not. On your birthday, wedding day or Christmas morning, even if you've only had a few hours' sleep you probably still wake up full of energy and enthusiasm. That's because the beliefs you hold about your sleep play such an important role in how you feel when you wake up.

How can you stop wasting your life and start claiming your ultimate potential? One way to turn things around is to change the way you think and feel about having a morning and evening practice.

YOUR TIME IS NOW

"By making the decision to have a morning and evening practice, you're taking control of your life, one day at a time."
—MARIANA ARDELEAN

Set your intention for the day

> *Intention is more than wishful thinking— it's willful direction. It is a philosophy of the heart put into practice, a consistency of conscious patterns of thought, energy and action. Through intention, we see more and create with more clarity, passion, and authenticity. Our attention then becomes a spotlight for every shred of supporting evidence that we're on the right path.*
>
> —Jennifer Williamson

Plan the day. Work out exactly what you will be doing by setting your intention for the day. As Wayne Walter Dyer the motivational speaker and self-help author said: "Our intention creates our reality" because "you create your thoughts, your thoughts create your intentions and your intentions create your reality."

Decide when you will finish work, according to your current commitments and appointments. When you do this, you will find yourself being more intentional and staying on the path because you have scheduled what's important into your practice.

There is an interesting statement: 'Work expands to fill the time available for its completion.' This statement was made by Cyril Northcote Parkinson, the famous British historian and author, in 1955, and first appeared in an article for *The Economist*. It later became the focus of one of Parkinson's books, *Parkinson's Law: The Pursuit of Progress*.

By planning and setting your intention for when you will complete a specific task, you're taking all the necessary steps to ensure it will be done within the set timeframe.

Once you have set the intention for your day, it's time for meditation.

Meditation

> *The things that trouble our spirits are within us already. In meditation, we must face them, accept them, and set them aside one by one.*
> —Christopher L Bennett

When you pay attention to your thoughts and are able to integrate those thoughts into your stream of consciousness, you experience the present moment. The word for meditation in Tibetan is *gom*, which means 'to familiarise'. Familiarise yourself with a positive state of mind by training your mind to become clear so that you can concentrate on what you want.

Pay attention to the present moment; this is where your life exists. You're not aiming for ten minutes in the past or even ten minutes in the future. You're aiming for *this*

YOUR TIME IS NOW

moment, right now, because that's all you have. There's no point in thinking about what happened ten days ago, or being concerned about what's going to happen in ten days' time. There's no need to do that because all you have is this moment. This moment right now.

If you're like most people, your mind probably wanders all over the place, veering from one thought to another. You might be at work, but you're thinking: *I need to call my husband. I need to stop to get some milk. What shall I cook for dinner?* You might be at home with your children, partner or husband, but you're thinking: *I forgot to contact my client. I need to contact that supplier. I'd love to have a holiday.* Your mind is in a state the Buddha called 'monkey mind'. That's being human.

Some thoughts may trigger frustration or fear, or even make you feel overwhelmed. That's when you're likely to experience automatic reaction. When someone cuts you off in traffic, you might lose your cool, swear or otherwise react negatively to the situation. But if you do that, you have lost control of the situation. Your thoughts and emotions have reacted to the situation, and you have given away your power by doing that. Suddenly you feel powerless.

If you train yourself true meditation, you can choose to respond instead of reacting to a situation, which means

MEDITATION

that you hold onto your power. By choosing consciously, you have the ability to direct your thoughts; this is what you practise during meditation. As it becomes a practice, it will also become integrated with who you really are. As you incorporate this into your daily life, you will gain the ability to direct your focus and respond to circumstances rather than reacting to them and living on autopilot.

When you react, the reaction is a survival and defence mechanism that does not take into consideration long-term consequences or regret. When you respond, you notice the reaction, you pause, you take a breath and you assess the situation as you allow the emotional reaction to pass.

Viktor E Frankl, the Austrian neurologist, psychiatrist and Holocaust survivor, said, 'Between stimulus and response there is a space. In that space is a power to choose our response. In our response lies our growth and our freedom.'

Meditation will teach you to choose where to focus your energy as you respond rather than react to what's coming your way. As you do that, you can tap into the present moment where gratitude, love, joy and a sense of calm live. In those moments, you can transform and establish profound wisdom, understanding and insight.

You can acknowledge your conscious thoughts and let them go, and as you do you will have a true sense of peace and calmness. You can also change your emotions and unconscious thoughts if you choose to.

Meditation is a popular technique that many people in highly demanding jobs use to fight stress and to feel better within themselves. Over the years, brain research has provided us with evidence of something that practitioners of meditation have maintained for centuries: if you practise meditation on a regular basis, you will reach a sense of peace and a different level of awareness.

Over the past thirty years, more than a thousand research studies have been conducted on the effects of meditation at different universities and research institutes all over the world. Many of those studies, which have been published in major scientific journals, have shown the importance of the practice.

Like most people, you probably feel stressed, frustrated and overwhelmed at times. Practising silence in the morning when you wake up, and in the evening before you go to bed will also help you feel calmer and less stressed.

The Huffington Post reported that Oprah Winfrey believes that transcendental meditation has helped her

MEDITATION

'connect with that which is God'. Other well-known people, such as Sting, Jerry Seinfeld, Russell Simmons, Katy Perry, Hugh Jackman, Rupert Murdoch, Sheryl Crow, Russell Brand, David Lynch, Clint Eastwood and Shirley MacLaine have also stated that meditation is an essential part of their life.

How can you introduce meditation into your morning and evening routines, or even during the day if you choose to? Before you start your meditation session, take a break from your worry, and as you do so concentrate only on your breathing. Find a quiet, comfortable place to sit, for instance on a cushion or on the couch. Sit upright, roll your shoulders back and your chest slightly forward so you can stretch your spine.

Now close your eyes, or look at the wall in front of you. Bring your attention to your breath, inhaling through your nose and exhaling through your mouth. Breathe slowly, into your belly and not your chest. Set a pace for your breath. For instance, breathe in for three seconds, then breathe out for three seconds. Try not to push away any thoughts, but if they come, simply acknowledge them and gently bring your focus back on your breathing.

At first this may be challenging, but it will gradually become more comfortable and natural, especially if you practise on a regular basis. Day by day, you'll feel your stress levels reduce.

The easiest way to de-stress fast and re-centre yourself is to 'take six'. Take six deep rhythmic breaths in through your nose, and then breathe out through your mouth, as though you were blowing through a straw.

If paying attention to your breath is not for you, you could try guided meditation. This is where a trained professional can take you through the process, either in person or via a recording that can be accompanied by soft music in the background.

At first I really struggled with meditation; I was unable to concentrate, and my mind wandered all over the place. Over time, I tried different types of meditation, followed different mentors, and had background music or no music. To start with I followed Bob Proctor, then Vishen Lakhiani's six-phase meditation, then John Assaraf, then Gabrielle Bernstein, and more recently Dr Joe Dispenza. Finally I found a few types of meditation that I now use on a regular basis. I highly recommend the app Headspace, Insight Timer and Calm—Meditation and Sleep.

If you have already attempted similar techniques in the past and found they were not for you, try exploring other types of meditation before dismissing the practice.

MEDITATION

Meditation is an excellent way to relax and re-centre yourself.

Benefits of meditation

There are many different types of meditation: compassion, mindfulness, mantra-based, love and kindness. While the aim of each type of meditation may be different, they all offer universal benefits. Those benefits include a reduction in stress, insomnia and anxiety; improved concentration; greater self-esteem; adoption of a healthy lifestyle; an increase in self-awareness, happiness, acceptance and creativity; improved relationships; creating/manifesting; and a slowing down of biological aging.

Also, the practice of meditation will benefit your cardiovascular and immune systems through your inner calmness and ability to relax as you centre yourself in the here and now. When you're not paying attention to what was, and not worrying about what could be, you will stay grounded in the present moment and notice the now.

You probably find yourself thinking about other things often, and missing the current moment, the current reality. If you go on holiday, you might be thinking about what's happening at home or work. When you spend time with your family, you might be daydreaming about your next holiday.

Like most people, you're probably busy, and worried about the future instead of being in the here and now. When you spend time with your children, husband, partner, friends or colleagues, *be* with them. Be present. They will never forget how you made them feel. You're in control; you can respond and be present to claim your ultimate potential.

Centre Yourself Meditation

This simple meditation will give you the ability to stay cool, and help you focus your attention and energy on things that are productive and powerful. Begin with your palms facing outwards and your shoulders rolled back. Straighten up your spine. With your eyes open or closed, stay totally relaxed and comfortable. Take a slow, deep breath through your nose and exhale through your mouth as though you were blowing through a straw.

Three, two, one ...

MEDITATION

Take a gentle deep breath in through your nose and out through your mouth. And again. Take a gentle deep breath in through your nose and out through your mouth. Do this at your own pace.
Take a deep breath in through your nose and out through your mouth, as though you were blowing through a straw. And again.
Take a deep breath in through your nose and out through your mouth.
Take a deep breath in through your nose and out through your mouth.
Take a deep breath in through your nose and out through your mouth.

As you become even more relaxed, keep breathing through your nose and out through your mouth. Release any stress or doubts.

Practise this breathing exercise throughout the day and notice how calm you become. And as you do this, repeat to yourself:

I breathe in love, I breathe out stress.
I breathe in love, I breathe out stress.
I breathe in love, I breathe out stress.
I breathe in love, I breathe out stress.

YOUR TIME IS NOW

I breathe in love, I breathe out stress.
I breathe in love, I breathe out stress.

I breathe in calmness, I breathe out self-doubt.
I breathe in calmness, I breathe out self-doubt.
I breathe in calmness, I breathe out self-doubt.
I breathe in calmness, I breathe out self-doubt.
I breathe in calmness, I breathe out self-doubt.
I breathe in calmness, I breathe out self-doubt.

I breathe in calmness, I breathe out worry.
I breathe in calmness, I breathe out worry.
I breathe in calmness, I breathe out worry.
I breathe in calmness, I breathe out worry.
I breathe in calmness, I breathe out worry.
I breathe in calmness, I breathe out worry.

I breathe in peace, I breathe out fear.
I breathe in peace, I breathe out fear.
I breathe in peace, I breathe out fear.
I breathe in peace, I breathe out fear.
I breathe in peace, I breathe out fear.
I breathe in peace, I breathe out fear.

I breathe in calmness, I breathe out overwhelm.

MEDITATION

I breathe in calmness, I breathe out overwhelm.
I breathe in calmness, I breathe out overwhelm.
I breathe in calmness, I breathe out overwhelm.
I breathe in calmness, I breathe out overwhelm.
I breathe in calmness, I breathe out overwhelm.

As you come out of this meditation, wiggle your toes and wiggle your fingers... and slowly start moving... and when you're ready gently open your eyes and come back to now.

According to researchers, when you're in a state that disempowers you emotionally or financially, your stress centre becomes activated, which lowers your brain function. As you take six rhythmic breaths, you deactivate your stress response, and that allows you to be calm and in a good frame of mind

For the next few minutes, just breathe, relax and enjoy being calm, feeling inner peace as you breathe, because this is your time.

Guided Meditation

Find a comfortable space. Don't worry about being in a quiet area. Wearing comfortable clothing, settle into a relaxed position. It's best to sit upright, with your back supported and your head free. Comfort is the key. I'll be with you and guiding you every step of the way.

Focus on your breath. If you have any thoughts, don't worry because thoughts are not the enemy. You can go ahead and close your eyes if you haven't done so already. As you do that, gently place your awareness on your breath. Inhale through your nose and exhale through your mouth, as though you're blowing through a straw. Remain conscious of your breathing in and breathing out.

When thoughts come, and they will, visualise them as clouds passing in the sky. Notice your thoughts, and as you do, let them float away and return to focusing on your breath. Maintain a sense of calmness by continuing to follow your breath.

Breathe in calmness, breathe out stress.
Breathe in peace, breathe out stress.

And again.

Breathe in calmness, breathe out stress.
Breathe in peace, breathe out stress.

MEDITATION

As you do this, feel the air that you're inhaling and exhaling, as it passes through your nostrils, going down to your chest like a cool breeze. With each breath, feel the calmness and release the stress. Inhale peace, exhale fear. Inhale calmness, exhale frustration. Let all negativity be released. Your body unwinds as you're letting go. White light surrounds you. Keep refocusing on your breath and the calmness that surrounds you.

As you come out of this meditation, wiggle your toes and your fingers and slowly start moving and when you're ready gently open your eyes and come back to now.

Much love and gratitude and continue to connect with who you truly are.

And before you get up to get on with your day take a moment to acknowledge yourself and stay here, be here, simply being for as long as you like, knowing that you can take this with you within your day, as this is your time.

Now let's move on to visualisation.

YOUR TIME IS NOW

"*Take a moment to acknowledge yourself and connect with who you truly are.*"
—MARIANA ARDELEAN

Visualisation

> *To accomplish great things we
> must first dream, then visualize,
> then plan ... believe ... act!*
> **—Alfred A Montapert**

What is visualisation? Visualisations are images that are created in the mind's eye. Your brain remembers everything you see or imagine on a regular basis. The smile of a special person in your life, a car that stands out to you, or something you might be interested in doing or daydreaming about it, like lying down on a beach on a secluded island.

When you daydream, you can replay those images in your mind over and over and over again, as many times as you want. Your unconscious mind will register

YOUR TIME IS NOW

those images just as powerfully as if they were things you had actually seen, even though they exist only in your imagination. To your unconscious mind, the images are real because your unconscious mind is unable to differentiate between reality and imagination.

By using visualisation, you can create the reality that you desire deep within you by imagining what you really want. When you visualise something over and over again, you can actually accelerate the neural connections in your brain much faster than if you were experiencing an actual event.

One person may not be able to actually 'see' a mental movie in their mind's eye the way someone else can. Instead, they might experience a strong feeling, a significant sound or taste, or a powerful emotion. That's okay.

You may be wondering how this all works. As you know, seeing and feeling is believing. You believe what you see and what you actually feel. Whether you actually see something or only imagine seeing something, on an unconscious level your brain registers that as being real. When you create an image on the screen of your mind's eye, your brain begins to believe that it actually happened or is happening now. On an unconscious level, that specific event that you have imagined has actually taken place.

VISUALISATION

Visualisation is an important tool that you have at your disposal that will help you to reach your ultimate potential. Visualisation is a technique that is used by many professional athletes. You, too, can use this technique to visualise your ideal day, or life, or dreams, desires and goals.

Not that long ago, I read about an experiment that was carried out with high school basketballers. The experiment was intended to improve their basketball foul shots.

First, the whole team was tested for accuracy on their foul shots, and then the class was divided into two groups. The first group was asked to practise foul shots on the court every day. The second group was also asked to practise foul shots, but in an entirely different way; they never touched a basketball and never practised on the actual court. They could practise at home while resting, or travelling on the train, everywhere but on the court. You might be wondering how they were able to practise at all.

The second group only *imagined* that they were doing foul shots. They visualised themselves making perfect foul shots every time they attempted them. They did that in their imagination again and again and again; they visualised the ball falling into the basket perfectly every time, to the point that they actually heard the *swish* of the net. The only thing this group didn't do is imagine they had made a mistake, or that the ball didn't fall through the basket perfectly; they imagined that it went through perfectly every time.

After two weeks, the two groups were tested again on the basketball court. After all their regular practice, the first group had improved their scores significantly, which was to be expected. Surprisingly, the second group had improved their scores by almost the same amount, and they had never even touched a basketball.

What this experiment shows is that visualisation can be as effective as actual physical activity when it comes to improving a skill. Visualisation is also known as 'mental rehearsal', but regardless of what it is called, it's the same basic technique. It's the process of creating a mental image or intention of what you want to happen, and what you want to feel, and treating those things as if they were an actual reality.

Most elite athletes routinely use visualisation techniques as part of their training and competition routines. There have been many stories over the years of high-performance athletes who have used this type of technique to improve their skill and mental awareness, as

VISUALISATION

well as increase their sense of wellbeing and confidence within themselves.

Athletes use this technique to see the outcome of a game or race, or the outcome of a training session in the way they want to perform. They imagine the desired outcome. They see themselves stepping into the feeling, to the point that they can even hear the crowd cheering. They visualise every detail, including the way they feel about performing a specific task. By using their mind, and visualising the desired state, they can recall images again and again, enhancing their skills through repetition.

Mental rehearsal is similar to physical practice; the only real difference is that mental practice is carried out in the mind. By doing the practice repeatedly, athletes are training their bodies to perform, in reality, the skills they have only imagined up to that point.

You, too, can improve any skill, but you need to practise and rehearse on a regular basis.

You can try a similar experiment with yourself. Take a rubbish bin and some scrunched-up paper. Place the rubbish a set distance away from you and toss the paper towards it, aiming to get it in the bin. You will miss some of the time, and some of the time you will get the paper in the bin. Practise a few times to ensure that you are far enough away from the bin.

Now, remember one of the ways that you missed. Picture in your mind's eye, as clearly as you can, exactly what happened to the scrunched-up paper. See the paper miss the bin and fall on the floor. Hold that memory in your mind.

Throw the paper at least seven more times, keeping track of how many times you get it in the bin and how many times you missed.

Now change your memory picture to one of the best shots that you've made. Choose one of the most recent throws you made, where you scored a perfect hit. Focus on that image.

Now throw another seven scrunched-up pieces of paper. I would be surprised if you didn't find that your score has actually improved. Your score will continue to improve if you continue with this experiment.

By using the same principles, you can learn to use mental rehearsal to realise positive solutions to any problems you're facing. You can use it to realise opportunities for yourself. It's one of the best tools you can use to help you accomplish your goals.

You can control your visualisation and imagination to achieve the desired results. So far, I have used

VISUALISATION

visualisation and imagination of things that I have actually seen before. In other words, things that I am remembering. If you have never seen something before, you have to imagine it. You can learn to project your visualisation as well as your imagination. Imagine seeing yourself in a picture that is in front of you and a little higher than where you are. In other words, to see this picture you need to look a little higher than your line of sight when you're visualising it.

What you're actually doing is projecting this picture into your mind's eye. You're imagining it, visualising it. You can influence this with your energy once the picture has the exact detail that you want it to have. It will eventually manifest into your physical world. As you bring it forward, you will attract the things you need to make it a reality.

This is where everything comes from. Everything around you was created twice, once as a thought, or mental picture, and once as a physical reality. You can use this to set goals. Achieve your goals by visualising them and programming your mind to turn your visions into reality. Focus your thoughts so you can achieve what you desire.

It's important to visualise the goal and what you want to achieve. Your mind doesn't know or care whether you're actually practising or only imagining that you're practising. The actual benefit will be the same. To your mind, the physical activity and the imaginary activity are the same.

Researchers are finding that, in certain circumstances, physical and psychological reactions can be improved through visualisation. Repeated visualisation builds confidence, along with the ability to perform specific skills under pressure in a variety of different situations.

Many Olympic athletes have specific visualisation techniques that result in very vivid experiences in which they have complete control over their performance. They believe in themselves and what they are capable of. Guided visualisation and mental rehearsal can maximise the effectiveness and efficiency of their training.

Nicole Detling, sports psychologist and assistant professor at the University of Utah, has worked with the United States Olympic team. She said, 'The more an athlete can imagine the entire package, the better it's going to be.'

While you're visualising, you can use all of your senses—sound, sight, smell, taste and touch—to make this tool even more powerful.

The best time to do visualisation is either while you're doing your meditation, or straight after you finish

VISUALISATION

your meditation. That's when your body and your mind are deeply relaxed. Your brain-wave pattern actually changes and becomes slower in this state. Alpha is when you have a lower level of brain waves. At this level, there is an increased level of serotonin production and higher intuition. This is where you can begin to access your unconscious mind; it's similar to pre-waking or pre-sleep drowsiness.

Your brain-wave pattern changes to beta waves when you're busy and consciously undertaking any activity.

Researchers have found that alpha brain waves are the heart state of consciousness, due to the relaxing effect they have on the mind and body, and that there is no better time to create change through the use of visualisation.

So if you visualise in a deeply relaxed state, you will be able to make far more effective changes in your life than when you're thinking or planning in an active state. While meditating in the alpha state, as you relax every muscle in your body and feel gratitude, you're at your most receptive to receiving suggestions for change.

When you first start out, you may not actually be able to envision anything when you try to imagine it. That's okay. There's nothing wrong with you. Some people see blurry images, while others see sharp, vivid images. And there are some who feel it, getting a sense for the thing that they want. This is all fine. Some people are orientated visually, and so are more likely to see something. Others are more kinaesthetically orientated, and likely to feel more. Those who are more receptive to auditory input may hear something instead.

If you're still not sure about it, or can't think of what to visualise, just close your eyes, relax and think of something that you're familiar with. You could think of your bedroom, living room or front door. Remember some familiar details. Think of the colours. Imagine walking into your bedroom and lying on the bed, sitting down on your couch, or walking through your front door. Recall a pleasant memory you have experienced in each of those spaces. For instance, how did you feel when you sat down on the couch? How did you feel when you walked through the door?

Remember and enjoy the experience as vividly as possible so you can enjoy those sensations again. Use whatever works for you to bring any of those sensors within your mind and use them in your process of visualisation. Creative visualisation generally comes naturally to most people, since we tend to think in pictures. The more you practise, the easier it will get.

VISUALISATION

Basic steps to effective visualisation:

1. Decide what you would like to visualise. This could be in any area of your life. It could be finances, health, family or work. The important thing is that you pick something simple, something you think you will be able to achieve and won't feel any resistance to. This should give you the feeling you need for creative visualisation, and the experience will work for you. Once you've been practising for a while, you can attempt more challenging issues that you would like to be resolved.
2. Create a picture. Feel it. Believe that what you want is something you already have. Think of it in the present tense; it already exists. Bring your emotions into it, specifically the feeling of being grateful. Think, see, feel and hear it exactly the way you want it. It has already happened. Imagine yourself in that specific situation. Look at it and sense it as if you have it now.
3. Focus on that picture. Bring the idea and your mental picture to mind as often as you can, especially first thing in the morning and before you go to bed. If possible, see if you can do this throughout the day. By doing so, the picture will become integrated with who you are, a part of your life as it becomes your

reality. Focus on this in a relaxed state of mind, and a state of expectation.
4. Give this picture a positive energy. Feel gratitude, because you already have it. You're happy. You see yourself as having achieved it already. Imagine what you're telling yourself, what others are telling you. Practise the feeling and being in that state. Practise this until you achieve your desired outcome.
5. At the end of any visualisation process you can add: 'This or something better.' This is a statement of intention, surrender, acceptance and expectancy. When you least expect it, something greater will come along. Once you achieve it, acknowledge yourself consciously, give yourself appreciation for it and thank God, the universe, or your higher spirit for fulfilling your request.

If for any reason you find it challenging to practise visualisation, you can use affirmations instead. As an example, if you want to write a book, you can visualise yourself feeling inspired and joyfully writing page after page after page at your desk, in the garden or anywhere else where you think and feel, and where you see yourself being inspired. Alternatively, you can use affirmations. Say to yourself: 'I am inspired and joyfully

VISUALISATION

writing page after page.' Your affirmations can help you visualise the answers when you ask yourself questions such as: *What do I want? Why do I want it? What am I committed to doing to get there?*

Sir Isaac Newton said, 'If I have seen further than other men it is because I have stood on the shoulders of giants.' Give yourself permission to visualise an extraordinary life in your mind's eye. Stand on the shoulders of those you admire. Take action and follow through with your plans. By doing this on a regular basis you will get to your desired destination and claim your ultimate potential.

YOUR TIME IS NOW

Give yourself permission to visualise an extraordinary life.
—**MARIANA ARDELEAN**

Affirmations

It's the repetition of affirmations that leads to belief. And once that belief becomes a deep conviction, things begin to happen.
—Claude M Bristol

What are affirmations specifically? Why use affirmations? An affirmation is simply a statement written in the first person. It's a short statement that creates change, feelings and emotions in the person who uses it. Because, feelings are the language of the mind, and emotions are the language of the body. Feelings occur on a conscious level, whereas emotions can occur on an unconscious level and usually occur first. Emotions are observable physical states that arise because of a stimulus. Feelings are mental associations and reactions to emotions, and they can be hidden.

The purpose of an affirmation is to inspire you as well as remind you of what's possible. An affirmation is a strong, positive statement confirming that something is already so. It's making a firm statement to show that you believe whatever you imagine is already there. To affirm means 'to make firm'. You can use affirmations to focus on yourself as well as your goals, and to encourage yourself to make positive changes in your life.

Like most people, you probably carry on a continuous inner dialogue with yourself, inside of your mind. You have thoughts and ideas, and most of the time you're probably not even consciously aware of all of your thoughts, what you're telling yourself. That inner dialogue actually forms the basis of how you shape your experiences and your reality. The internal dialogue influences how you feel, your prescription and what actually happened in reality.

Your thoughts ultimately attract and create everything that happens around you. Perception is the interpretation, or sensory input, gathered by the five senses: smell, touch, hearing, vision and taste. This is done on a cognitive level and it's how we create meaning from our surroundings and ourselves.

AFFIRMATIONS

Those who practise meditation would have noticed that sometimes it can be quite challenging to connect with the inner intuitive self. Traditional meditation is simply observing your inner dialogue, and this allows you to become consciously aware of your thoughts.

Your thoughts are like old patterns in your life. They represent old programming you have picked up since you were a child, which is possibly still influencing what is happening to you today. By observing this, you may find that you habitually have thoughts like: *I'm not good enough. That's not going to work out.*

Knowing this, you can turn things around.

People use affirmations for many different reasons. Firstly, they can be used to reprogram the subconscious mind and encourage belief in your ability. Secondly, you can use affirmations to create the reality you want, especially when it comes to fulfilment, beliefs, love and wealth.

Using affirmations is a powerful technique, one that can transform your life in a very short period. You can change your attitude and expectations about life, and improve what you want to create for yourself. You can make affirmations in silence, you can read them, you can write them, you can chant them, and you can even sing them. You can use affirmations in the morning, during the day and in the evenings as you start creating your ideal life.

According to Walter E Jacobson MD, affirmations play a significant role, especially when it comes to reprogramming the unconscious mind with what we really want to believe on an unconscious level, as well as the desires we have for our lives.

Speaking affirmations aloud can be a powerful method of self-communication. All the 'I' and 'I am' affirmations that you think and speak out loud determine your success or failure in life.

You may ask what the secret is to putting together an effective affirmation. Usually, affirmations start with 'I' or 'I am', followed by a statement. Simply using 'I' or 'I am' turns the information into a statement of identity. The most powerful statements you can make are identity statements, 'I am' statements, such as 'I am broke' or 'I am wealthy'. What you believe is what your subconscious will take as evidence of truth. You're in control of your consciousness, and can influence the subconscious by creating your own identity statements.

When it comes to identity affirmations, the words that follow the 'I' and 'I am' determine the kind of life you will live:

AFFIRMATIONS

- I am happy.
- I am grateful.
- I am determined.
- I am calm.
- I am powerful.

Or:

- I am depressed.
- I am stressed.
- I am overweight.
- I am angry.
- I am weak.

Being mindful, and knowing that you can choose what follows after the 'I am' means that you're empowering yourself. You can choose what you really want to experience in your life to claim your ultimate potential.

Personally, I like to use Bob Proctor's 'I am' statements, such as 'I am so grateful and happy now that ...', completing the affirmation with what you desire. For instance, you could say, 'I love myself and who I am.'

It's important to use the present tense for affirmations and goals as this tells the unconscious mind that something has already happened; that it already is. Also, affirmations must be positive as opposed to negative. It's important to include feelings and emotions in your affirmations because you will be able to associate with those emotions and feelings to experience the statements.

Write the affirmations as if they have already happened. This means saying, 'I am an experienced public speaker,' rather than, 'After I've practised for three more months I will become an experienced public speaker.'

Many people feel a bit silly at first when they say an affirmation they don't actually believe, that which hasn't happened yet. The important thing to remember is that affirmations are designed to reprogram your subconscious mind, even though on a conscious level you may not believe what you're saying.

Also, it's important to remember how the subconscious mind works and the significance of retraining your brain. Your subconscious mind is unable to differentiate between what's real and what's not real, and it will accept everything you give it.

It's essential to read your affirmations first thing in the morning when you wake up and just before you go to bed in the evening, as this will help reprogram your subconscious mind. Also, suggestions have been made

AFFIRMATIONS

by multiple experts that updating your affirmation on a regular basis and associating emotions with it will help you move forward to your desired outcome. This is something personal, however, and only you know what you want and how you feel about it.

You can also put affirmations as sticky notes on the mirror in the bathroom so you see them first thing in the morning. You can have them at work, or in your wallet. Place them anywhere that you will actually see and read them. Writing down your affirmations on a regular basis is also useful, because the simple fact that you're writing them down is another way of making the affirmations part of your subconscious mind.

Most people read their affirmations rather than write them, and that's okay. Others choose to have them printed on cards and keep them in their pocket. You could also use different apps, such as Thing Up. With this app, you can record your affirmation in your own voice, or you can use the pre-sets to record anything you want. You can also choose to have background music or not. It makes it easy to listen to yourself every morning and evening, and of course during the day, or even while you're driving.

You may be wondering how you go from an ordinary life to a life that you love, one that truly fulfils you. As previously mentioned, one way is to look at your self-talk.

You have been subconsciously programmed to talk to yourself in a certain way, but it's possible to change this. By choosing to be persistent, and by using positive affirmations, you can slowly claim your ultimate potential.

Like everyone, you have a constant stream of thoughts in your head that are based on your previous experiences. Your thoughts can work for or against you, depending on how you use them. To turn some of your ideas into positive affirmations is just a matter of following a few simple steps.

Start by clearly writing down how you want your life to look in every area. Clarify your motives by asking yourself why you want this. Ask yourself what you're prepared to do to get your life there, or even just to get to the next level.

Examples of affirmations:

- I am grateful for what life has to offer.
- What I see in others I also see within myself.
- I am grateful for my ability to acknowledge myself and others.

AFFIRMATIONS

- I am so grateful and happy now that I have opportunities to help others fulfil their inspired dreams.
- I am learning to grow and am moving forward every day.
- I am nourishing my mind with inspiring thoughts.
- What I can conceive and believe, I can achieve.
- I love the person I'm becoming.
- I love and accept myself unconditionally.
- I approve of myself and feel great about myself.
- I visualise the achievement of my goals on a daily basis.
- I accomplish everything I set out to do.
- I plan my work.
- I am healthy and wealthy.
- I am so grateful and happy now that I'm attracting healthy and amazing people into my life.
- I have infinite potential.
- I am a genius, and I believe in my skills and my abilities.
- I am acknowledging myself and my work, and my self-confidence is rising.
- I am worthy of all the things that happen in my life.

- I am letting go of the negative feelings about myself and accept the good in my life.
- I will stand by my decisions.
- I am happy and grateful now for all the opportunities in my life.
- I am healthy, happy and prosperous.
- I am generous, and the more I give the more I receive.
- I value my time and I am wealthy.
- I am open to receiving abundance.
- I am prosperous.
- I am magnetic, and I have attracted amazing people.
- I am a natural-born leader.
- I love what I do, and I do what I love.
- I follow my intuition and my heart.
- I prioritise my day and focus on my priorities.

Here is an example of a famous affirmation by Emil Coue: 'Day by day, in every way, I am getting better and better.'

According to Napoleon Hill, in his book *Think and Grow Rich*, unless you believe that what you're affirming will happen, you will not achieve your desired outcome.

AFFIRMATIONS

The most important thing to do after you have created an affirmation is to be sure to read it out loud to yourself at least twice a day, once in the morning and again just before you go to bed. Affirmations and visualisations are powerful tools, and by using them consciously you can unlock and claim your ultimate potential.

Visualising the life of your dreams, and affirming it to yourself, will change the perspective you have on your daily routine.

YOUR TIME IS NOW

"Your inner dialogue forms the basis of how you shape your experiences and your reality."
—MARIANA ARDELEAN

Exercise

> *To enjoy the glow of good health, you must exercise.*
> —**Gene Tunney**

Most people know the importance of exercise, yet far too many people don't exercise on a regular basis. Plato said, 'For a man to succeed in life, God provided him with two means, education and physical activity. Not separately, one for the soul and the other for the body, but the two together. With those two means, man can attain perfection.' Your body and mind need to be in tune for you to have the ability to function and reach your ultimate potential.

Hippocrates of Kos (ca 460–370 BC), a physician in ancient Greece, is considered one of the most outstanding figures in history. He is known as the 'father of medicine'. He recognised the importance of exercise around 300 BC, when he said, 'If you are in a bad mood go for a walk. If you are still in a bad mood go for another walk.'

Exercise regulates emotions, reduces stress and anxiety, boosts mood, generates a sense of wellbeing, and optimises cognitive function. Being consistent and having a daily routine is important. Consistency is a conscious choice, and it requires will and determination because it often takes time for exercise to become a habit. A new habit also creates new pathways in the brain.

Our hunter-gatherer ancestors were required to have a certain standard of fitness for their survival. If they could not run and hunt, they did not eat. These days most of us don't have to hunt, but our genes haven't changed much over the years. On the other hand, our brains have evolved, and we can plan to learn, to imagine, and to avoid consequences so we can become the best versions of ourselves.

The Mayo Clinic has looked at over 1600 scientific-paper reviews which show that exercise improves the brain. It can prevent cognitive decline, and lessen the threat of Alzheimer's disease. It improves mood, energy and motivation at any age.

EXERCISE

Paul Dudley White, a physician known as the father of American cardiology, said, 'A vigorous five-mile walk will do more good for an unhappy but otherwise healthy adult than all the medicine and psychology in the world.'

Researchers at Duke University have shown the importance of exercise in the treatment of depression. In 1999, a double-blind study was conducted with 156 patients who were depressed and sedentary. They were divided into three categories. The first group was given exercise for forty minutes, three times a week. The second group was given the medication Zoloft. And the third group was given exercises plus Zoloft. After four months the results were amazing. The study concluded that exercise was as effective as antidepressants.

In an interview, James Blumenthal, the lead researcher in the study, said, 'One of the conclusions we can draw from this is that exercise may be just as effective as medication and may be a better alternative for certain patients.'

At the time, pharmaceutical companies complained that the study did not have a placebo group. The same researchers at Duke University did a follow-up study in 2007, with 202 people with mild to moderate depression. They were placed in four groups. The first group was given a home-based exercise program with instructions to check in regularly with the researchers. The second group undertook supervised exercise. The third group was given 200 milligrams of Zoloft. The fourth group was given a placebo.

As with the previous study, this study also concluded that exercise was as effective as antidepressants.

Studies have been done with Boston marathon runners, and these have concluded that exercise raises endorphins. When you exercise, you're actually firing more nerve cells because you're using more muscles, and raising your levels of attention and concentration. During exercise, you also increase your level of oxytocin, known as the 'love hormone'. Oxytocin reverses the body's response to stress, creating a buffer against stress in the future. It also helps activate the neuroplasticity required for learning and the ability to make changes. It heals any wounds from previous relationships, and it helps rewire the brain.

Every time you exercise, it affects your executive function, which is located in the prefrontal cortex. This influences planning and organisation; working memory; and the ability to initiate or build responses, evaluate consequences, learn from mistakes and maintain focus.

The benefits of exercise:

EXERCISE

- Used in the treatment of attention deficit hyperactivity disorder (ADHD)
- Effects neurochemistry and increases norepinephrine, which affects concentration, alertness, energy, attention span, cognitive function, anxiety, impulse, and irritability
- Increases levels of serotonin, which affects obsession and compulsion, memory, appetite, sex, aggression, mood, cognitive function, anxiety impulse, and irritability
- Affects dopamine, which influences the pleasure reward, learning, motivation, drive, attention, mood, cognitive function, appetite, sex, and aggression

Studies have shown that the introduction of at least thirty minutes of regular exercise in schools can decrease disciplinary problems and promote the ability to think and socialise, as well as decrease disruptive behaviour.

It's well known that exercise is important in keeping the body healthy, yet far too few people manage to exercise during the day, even though most do understand its importance. Most of us are aware of the benefits of exercise, such as reduced risk of disease, fitness, and feeling fantastic because we are in shape, but we frequently push it to one side instead of making it a priority.

I know I'm guilty of this myself. Many people's lives are full of activities and they feel too exhausted to exercise. I know this from personal experience. After working on my feet all day, it's the last thing on my mind in the evening.

Why not set up a practice and start the day with some exercise so you get it out of the way before your day has properly begun?

Every time you move, you activate your thinking brain cells, and the more you use your brain, the more it acts like a muscle, and the better it gets. If you're inactive for a long period, your body becomes habituated to sitting still. It can take years for obesity, heart disease and type-2 diabetes to show themselves, so it's important to make a conscious decision to exercise and maintain that discipline for a lifetime.

If you're not used to exercising, or if you have irregular activities on a daily basis, start small. Be consistent so you can form the habit of being active and exercising on a regular basis. You could do something as simple as moving around every hour, taking the stairs instead of the elevator, or parking further away when you go shopping. Do some exercise while you're

EXERCISE

watching TV or listening to music. Go for a walk around the block at least three to four times a week. Join a gym. Join an exercise class. Join a yoga class. Find a friend who wants to exercise with you.

The important thing is to move away from a sedentary life because this increases the risk of disease with age.

In his research, Rudolph E Tanzi, professor of neurology at Harvard University and director of the Genetic and Ageing Research Unit at Massachusetts General Hospital, concluded that physical exercise consisting of eight to ten thousand steps per day is an essential benchmark for physical activity. You can use your smartphone, or you can buy a Fitbit, to keep track of the steps you take every day.

Most days are busy, and full of last-minute appointments and other important things that pop up without warning. By introducing morning exercise, you will keep your body healthy, and you will feel invigorated and look forward to the day ahead. Thirty-fifth American president John F. Kennedy, often known by his initials JFK, said, 'Physical fitness is not only one of the most important keys to a healthy body, it is the basis of dynamic and creative intellectual activity.' By making time for exercise as part of your morning practice, you can increase the level of fulfilment in your life and be closer to claiming your ultimate potential.

When asked in an interview what was his number one key to success, self-made multimillionaire Eben Pagan replied, 'Start every morning off with a personal success ritual.' He went on to emphasise the importance of morning exercise as part of his morning practice, making a point of explaining how exercise gets his heart rate up and his lungs filled with oxygen.

Reading

> *The more that you read, the more things you will know. The more that you learn, the more places you will go.*
> —Dr Seuss

By reading in the morning or evening, you will focus on your personal growth and further your career. We can all find a little time to read, and reading books on personal development is a fantastic way of gaining insight from others who have experienced fulfilment in a variety of different areas. There are many books covering every type of goal, from increasing your earnings, to improving your relationships, to building a business, to marketing and sales.

A good reading strategy is to schedule your reading time and aim for a minimum of five to ten pages per day. Choose what time of day you prefer to read, morning or night, and include this in your practice. If you schedule it, you will do it. At the end of the day, it has to suit you and your lifestyle. Mortimer J Adler, the American philosopher, educator, and popular author, said, 'Reading is a basic tool in the living of a good life.'

Aim for either ten to twenty minutes of reading per day, depending on your speed. Surprisingly, assuming each book averages 200 pages, this will add up to 1,825 or 3,650 pages a year, which means you'll be reading around nine or eighteen books every year.

By using a visual pacer, not only can you boost your reading speed but your focus as well. A visual pacer can be your finger or a pen. Try using your left hand. For most people, this will not be the hand they normally use. Even if you're left-handed, use your left hand because this will stimulate the right side of your brain, which is the creative and imaginative side. It will also improve your comprehension.

It might seem uncomfortable at first, as with anything done for the first time, and you might even feel that it slows you down. But by pushing through that initial

READING

stage, you will improve your speed-reading as well as your comprehension.

If you read on your computer, you can use the cursor. Your eyes will be attracted to the motion, and it will draw you through the words. Others may choose to read e-books on a tablet.

Science has proven that there is a brain-body connection. When using different parts of the body, we stimulate different parts of the brain. The left side of the brain is more logical, more word and language oriented. It uses more of a linear process, and for most people reading is a left-brain activity. The right side of the brain is more oriented towards creativity, imagination, visualisation, and emotion.

While reading, it's important to activate the right side of the brain and its functions so that you're not just *hearing* the words but also *experiencing* the words, too. By engaging both sides of the brain, highlighting important information, making notes on the pages, you will find it easier to recall and refer to the information at a later date without having to reread the whole page again.

In his book, *Keep Your Brain Alive*, Dr Lawrence Katz showed that research with seniors had positive results when they used the left hand to activate the right side of the brain. With simple lifestyle changes, such as brushing teeth, eating or writing with the opposite hand kept the brain active in people aged eighty and above.

I have noticed a similar thing in my patients, especially those over the age of seventy-five. Some people come in prepared to wait for their appointment by bringing a book to read, or a crossword or Sudoku to do. These people are generally more active, more connected with themselves, easy-going and optimistic, and look forward to what life has to bring. I have encountered patients at ninety-two still planning overseas holidays with optimism and enthusiasm. Joseph Addison, the English essayist, poet, playwright, and politician, said, 'Reading is to the mind what exercise is to the body.'

Forgiveness

> *To forgive is the highest, most beautiful form of love. In return, you will receive untold peace and happiness.*
> —**Robert Muller**

What is forgiveness, you may ask. According to the *Greater Good magazine*, psychology defines forgiveness as a conscious, deliberate decision to be able to release feelings or any resentment towards a person or a group of people who have harmed us, regardless of whether they actually deserve our forgiveness or not.

You may also ask what this has to do with fulfilment and claiming your ultimate potential, especially when you aim for the things you really desire. You might be determined, persistent, and willing to change as you work towards achieving your goals, but still not attaining what you desire. This could be because you are sabotaging yourself by resisting or procrastinating, or it could be that you're easily distracted.

On a conscious level, you know what you want, but deep down, on an subconscious level, you might be filled with guilt and shame. Rather than believing that you're deserving, you may think you're not worthy. All of this is happening on an subconscious level, without your conscious awareness, so you're not aware of it.

Your subconscious mind can sabotage your conscious efforts by generating resistance and confusion. Then your external world reflects your internal world, and you don't achieve your desired outcome. The only way to put an end to feelings of guilt and shame is by forgiving and loving yourself as well as others.

Acting with kindness toward others, offering support and assistance when they are needed, providing resources to help others navigate challenges in their lives will all increase your self-esteem. To further increase your self-esteem, avoid acting selfishly and instead think of others. Let go of judgement, resentment, anger and jealousy. If you do these things, consistently, without

FORGIVENESS

expecting anything in return, you alter the balance between the part of the brain that believes you're worthy and the part that believes you're worthless.

Gradually, your subconscious mind will start to believe you're good enough, worthy, and deserving of fulfilment in your life. Slowly, your subconscious mind will reduce its efforts to sabotage you and increase its effort to generate more fulfilment in your life.

It's also important that you forgive yourself for any perceived past transgressions, which will be deeply embedded in your subconscious mind. Unless you can find a way to forgive yourself, you will never be able to end the shame and guilt that is sabotaging you.

If you forgive others, you can forgive yourself; this is projection. What this means is that regardless of how badly other people behave, if you judge their behaviour negatively you're actually projecting onto them your own subconscious beliefs about yourself, and you're in fact judging yourself.

When you think that other people are guilty, rather than yourself, it takes your subconscious mind away from any bad feelings you have towards yourself. You may feel less guilty about yourself as a result of your projection. It's important to understand that this will not actually reduce the guilt and shame you feel, because guilt and shame are profoundly embedded in your subconscious mind, hidden from conscious awareness.

To be able to turn this around and use projection to your advantage, it's essential to understand that when you stop judging others and choose to forgive them instead, you're forgiving yourself. So, our projections onto them is another way of actually forgiving ourselves. By doing this, you empower yourself, and replace your self-sabotage with self-love, which means your subconscious mind will work with you rather than against you.

Over the years, scientists have accepted the truth that the mind moves the body. The functions of your body are governed and controlled by your thoughts, regardless of whether your thoughts are conscious or unconscious.

Forgiveness is one way that you can improve the way you see, feel and look at things. Forgiveness is a unique concept. It means *letting go* rather than holding onto things that bother you, including your decisions; the way others behave towards you; the way others have interacted with you, and whether or not others have offended you.

Forgiving yourself is crucial because you're unable to change what you have done. Guilt and resentment are destructive emotions that you need to understand, feel

FORGIVENESS

and let go of completely. Realising that what you did yesterday, a week ago, a month ago or five years ago cannot be changed means that you can move forward and forgive yourself. If someone has wronged you, don't hold onto resentment. Let it go, and keep in mind that it doesn't mean you're giving that person the opportunity to do it again. Your thoughts influence your emotions, and your emotions affect your body.

Most people may believe that procrastination is a lack of willpower, but research has shown that it's not a form of laziness at all but a coping mechanism for stress.

Timothy Pychyl, psychology professor at Carleton University, has been studying procrastination for more than twenty years. He has found that the main thing that drives procrastination is not avoidance of work but avoidance of stress. He states that procrastination is actually 'a subconscious desire to feel good right now', to feel a little relief from stress. Also, more often than not, when you procrastinate it's more likely that you will end up feeling even more stressed by putting things off instead of dealing with them. If you forgive yourself for your procrastination, however, you will be less likely to continue to procrastinate, and possibly change your life because you will choose to start doing things differently.

Timothy Pychyl has also conducted research regarding the concept of 'future self' versus 'present self'. Your future self is the person you want to become. Experiments revealed that when people were shown a photo of themselves that had been digitally altered to make them look older, they were more likely to start saving for their retirement.

This means that your 'future self' can give you the objectivity to push yourself in the present—and it's also a great coping mechanism for stress.

Another way of letting go is to do a visualisation exercise. Start by forgiving someone for something small, and then move onto forgiving someone for something more significant. (For an online version of this exercise, go to www.yourtimeisnow.com.au and download the forgiveness visualisation.)

Forgiveness Visualisation

Gently Close your eyes. Take in some deep breaths. Breathe deeply into your stomach. Place one hand on your stomach so you can feel your hand rising and falling with each breath. Breathe deeper than you normally do.

FORGIVENESS

Now breathe even deeper. Breathe into your stomach. Keep your eyes closed and see the person you're thinking of in front of you. Connect with the mistake that you believe that person has made. As you do, bring awareness to the emotions that come up for you. And as you do this, acknowledge them without trying to change any of them. Your mind will come up with thoughts and ideas, and that's okay. Whatever your mind says, just say thank you and go back to your stomach.

Take a deep breath in and think of yourself breathing into your stomach as you anchor yourself to your breath. Now look at the person. Connect with the mistakes you believe they have made. Say to yourself:

- I do not condone it.
- I do not agree with it.
- I want you to know that it's not okay.
- What happened is not okay.
- I'm not okay with what happened.

Continue to breathe. If there are any other statements you want to say, just say them and keep on breathing. Breath through your stomach.

Look at that person in your mind's eye. See what colour they are. If you tend towards feelings, take note of the feelings that come up for you. Tap into them. Take note of what you're feeling about it, thinking about it, and ask yourself how someone else might feel about it if it had been done to them.

Whatever comes up for you, invite that feeling into your body. It could be anger, sadness, frustration or anxiety. Whatever it is for you, just breathe it in. Know that whatever is present within you right now is okay. You can handle it, even though it may be unfamiliar to you or seem weird.

Keep breathing into your stomach. Big breath in, all the way into your stomach. Keep breathing into your stomach. Invite the feeling that's there, whatever it is, either a light feeling or an overwhelming feeling. Invite it in as though you want it to be there.

This might seem strange to you. Your brain may say crazy stuff. Just stay with the feeling. Say thank you and keep on breathing. Keep breathing into your stomach, where you feel that feeling fully. Invite it in. Imagine you're a scientist and you're studying this feeling in your body. Imagine you're wearing a scientist's white coat and you're exploring this feeling. Ask yourself:

- What shape is it?
- What colour is it?

FORGIVENESS

- What kind of movement does it have?
- What is its density?
- How heavy is it?
- Is it moving around in my body?

As you ask these questions, keep on breathing. Keep on breathing into your stomach, and as you do, notice how the feeling changes. Notice how it moves. Realise that you're okay. Realise that it's okay for you to feel this way; that it's a good thing. Invite in the realisation that sometimes it can be hard to feel things like this. Start to notice the compassion.

Sometimes this exercise can be challenging. Sometimes life can be hard and that's okay. Sometimes no one gets it, and that's also okay. Acknowledge that it can be a challenge and just notice what that feels like for you.

Keep breathing. Just keep breathing into your body. Breathe into your stomach.

Notice the person in front of you. *See* the person in front of you. Invite yourself to see the humanity in them. You've already told them that you don't agree with their decision. Just see the humanity in them. Acknowledge that the part of them that made a stupid mistake could also be a part of you. That may be a challenge, but acknowledge it.

YOUR TIME IS NOW

It will come like a little light. It will show itself as a white light that shines out of them, just a little bit. Focus on that light. Be patient. Notice how the light starts to get bigger. Notice how it starts to show itself more. It was there all along.

As you notice the light increasing in size, breathe in how you feel about that. Just breathe in whatever is coming up for you. It's important that you breathe past any resistance and accept it for what it is. If anything comes up that feels hard, just breathe. If it's challenging, if you feel as though you're not getting it, accept it as okay. Just breathe into your stomach and say it's okay.

Continue breathing. Imagine that you have created a blanket. It's a forgiveness blanket. Imagine that you're wrapping that person up in the forgiveness blanket. Notice your feelings. Notice if there's any resistance. If there is, that's okay. Take your time. You don't need to change anything. If there is resistance, it's there for a good reason. If there's no resistance, that's okay, too. Just breathe. Keep on breathing. Just breathe into your stomach and wrap the person up in the blanket.

Remember the action. It's just about dealing with the feeling, that's all. The lesson you can take away is that it wasn't okay and processing this will actually strengthen you emotionally. This will allow you to have a stronger

FORGIVENESS

and more compelling boundary, and you will be able to say no next time.

Notice how you're feeling right now. Breathe deeper into your stomach, and notice how you're feeling.

Slowly, whenever you're ready, as you're coming out of this visualisation wiggle your toes and wiggle your fingers and you can slowly, start moving and when you're ready gently open your eyes and come back to now. Start moving around slowly. Know that whatever's there is okay. If you have any residual feelings, that's okay. Just keep breathing through your stomach.

If you feel a sense of calmness, that's wonderful. Just keep breathing through your stomach. Know that whatever you're feeling is okay. Whatever is going on, whatever you're feeling, it's all normal. Just keep on breathing. And before you get up to get on with your day take a moment to acknowledge yourself and stay here, be here, simply being for as long as you like.

YOUR TIME IS NOW

"*Forgiveness is one way that you can improve the way you see, feel and look at things, because your thoughts influence your emotions, and your emotions affect your body.*"

—MARIANA ARDELEAN

Gratitude and Appreciation

> *Gratitude makes sense of our past, brings peace for today, and creates a vision for tomorrow.*
> **—Melody Beattie**

How is gratitude and appreciation useful? Robert A Emmons PhD, professor of psychology at the University of California, and his colleagues carried out studies that spanned more than a decade. More than a thousand people, aged from eight to eighty years of age, participated.

It was found that those who practise gratitude on a consistent basis benefit from having a strong immune system, are less bothered by aches and pains, have lower blood pressure, tend to exercise and take better care of their general health, have better sleep patterns, and wake up feeling more refreshed. On a psychological level, they have a higher level of positive emotions, are more alert, experience more joy and pleasure, and are more optimistic and happy. On a social level, they are more helpful, generous, compassionate, forgiving and outgoing, and they feel less lonely and isolated.

Gratitude allows us to acknowledge the present and magnifies our positive emotions. Researchers have shown that positive emotions actually wear off quite quickly as we adapt to the circumstances in our lives, and we no longer feel gratitude in the same way. If you buy a new car, at first you feel happy and grateful. But after you've been driving it for a while you don't feel quite as excited anymore because the car is no longer new and you have become used to it. If you buy a new house, for a while you feel happy and appreciative living in it. But over time you become used to it and you no longer feel the way you did when you first moved in.

By being grateful, you're able to appreciate things that you might otherwise take for granted. Gratitude can block negative emotions like envy, resentment and regret because you cannot be grateful and envious at the same time.

GRATITUDE AND APPRECIATION

Grateful people are more resistant to stress. Studies have shown that when someone is faced with a serious incident or trauma they will recover more quickly if they come from a place of gratitude. Also, grateful people have a higher sense of self-worth because they appreciate what others are doing for them, and they recognise the value in what they themselves bring as well.

Robert A Emmous PhD states that gratitude 'has the power to heal, energise and change lives'. The ability to maintain an attitude of gratitude, regardless of how challenging or difficult the circumstances of your life, means that you're more likely to be able to overcome any obstacles that come your way.

Consider the thought that there is no crisis without a blessing. The next time you face difficult circumstances, ask yourself what the blessing could be in that situation. By asking this simple question, you can transform your stress into fulfilment, which will bring some awareness into any challenging situation in your life.

Be grateful for the simple fact that you're breathing. Every time you take a breath, you inhale molecules from the air that include nitrogen and oxygen as well as water, carbon dioxide and other elements that help your body create new cell tissue that regenerates your whole body every seven to ten years. That's the miracle of life. This is something that you can be grateful for every single moment as you claim your ultimate potential.

Be grateful that you wake up each day. Be grateful that you can see. Be grateful that you can speak. Be grateful for small things you have that others may not have. Be grateful to have clean drinking water. Be grateful that you can enjoy a nice cup of coffee. Be grateful that you have a warm bed. Be grateful that you have a roof over your head. Be grateful for each day that you're alive. My mentor, Sharon Pearson, in her international bestseller *Ultimate You* wrote: 'Gratitude ... appreciation is a cultivated habit. We, and only we, can give ourselves this need. To feel appreciation is a choice, which can be practiced until it comes automatically.'

Gratitude is the key to living a wonderful life as you claim your ultimate potential.

There is so much negativity in the world. The daily news is almost always negative, whether it's a financial fear, a global conflict, health challenges or crime, we are constantly bombarded by negativity, to the point that even our thoughts become negative and we become full of doubt.

To counteract the constant negativity around you, it's essential that you have positive experiences in your life. Gratitude is one of the things you can use on a regular

GRATITUDE AND APPRECIATION

basis to sustain an ongoing sense of joy and fulfilment in your life. By using gratitude, you can have the sense of peace, joy, and fulfilment that you crave, as you claim your ultimate potential.

Like most people, you're probably your own worst critic. Negative self-talk can bring you to a place of fear, reluctance and resistance. Demonstrating gratitude for all that you are, and all that you have, is the pathway to fulfilment and personal success.

To be able to experience and sustain the benefits of gratitude, it's essential that you make a daily habit of incorporating gratitude into your daily practice. At the beginning and end of each day, think of three to five things that you're grateful for. What are you grateful for specifically? How grateful do you feel? Can you share that gratitude with someone?

Being able to share and celebrate the victories in your life, whether big or small, is an important step towards appreciating and acknowledging yourself. By doing this on a regular basis, you will increase your sense of self-worth and self-fulfilment, and you will begin to take action even in moments of uncertainty.

Coming from a place of gratitude and appreciation in the way you look at things will begin to shift, to the point that you will notice your behaviour starting to change. You will notice that you have more compassion and empathy. You will respond to circumstances in your life instead of reacting to them.

Your language reflects your thoughts, and your thoughts create your reality. By being grateful, you will feel blessed and fortunate. You will feel that you have the gifts and ability to live an abundant and fulfilled life. Less grateful people focus on lack, and continually complain about their circumstances. Once you train your mind to see goodness everywhere around you, you will start to notice kindness, and more of the same will show up in your life.

A study showed if people suffering from a neuromuscular disorder kept a gratitude journal for over two weeks, they experienced a significant increase in positive emotions, and felt more optimistic and connected to others, compared to the other people in the study who did not keep a gratitude journal. Time and time again, science has verified that, by practising and maintaining an attitude of gratitude, we can pass through challenging times in our lives much easier than if we don't have an attitude of gratitude.

During challenging periods in your life, when bad things happen, there will usually be a positive side to

GRATITUDE AND APPRECIATION

them. Think of the last time something bad happened, now ask yourself these questions:

What am I grateful for now that this has happened?

_____
_____
_____
_____

What strengths do I now have because of this particular experience?

_____
_____
_____
_____

How has this specific event equipped me to be able to deal with similar challenges in the future?

_____
_____
_____
_____

How have I benefited from this specific event?

_____
_____
_____
_____
_____

How have I changed my perspective because of this experience?

_____
_____
_____
_____
_____

In another study, 221 young adults were asked to keep a gratitude journal for three weeks. During that time, their sense of well-being and life satisfaction improved. Conversely, when they were asked to keep a daily list of any hassles in their lives and record how they coped with the stress, their day-to-day behaviour didn't improve.

GRATITUDE AND APPRECIATION

Research has shown that being grateful for something in the present moment—thinking of something to be grateful for, or someone to feel gratitude towards—activates brain cells that release neurochemicals that correlate with that specific activity or thought.

Every positive thought or memory, or feeling of gratitude and appreciation activates dopamine and serotonin, the feel-good chemicals. When you feel the emotion of gratitude, you release oxytocin. A good example of this is when you fall in love, or you feel extremely happy about something you have done or that someone has done for you.

When you want to experience certain emotions, you can train yourself to bring them up by carefully choosing your thoughts. Emotions give rise to feelings, and being aware of your emotions is important.

One of the best things you can do is to train yourself to learn to exchange one emotion for another. If you have disempowering emotions, you can suggest to yourself that instead you should feel intentionally grateful for something. By practising, you can learn to be in a state of gratitude even when you're going through a difficult time. You can consciously train to put yourself in a state of gratitude even when things are not going well for you.

To learn to develop this ability, you have to nurture it and practise on a regular basis.

Gratitude activates neurones of positivity. Gratitude activates neurones of possibility. Gratitude activates neurones of opportunity. Gratitude activates neurones of wellbeing.

It's too easy to see things in a negative light. You don't have that business yet. Or you do have the business but it's not growing at the rate you would like. You haven't lost the excess weight yet. Your relationship is not working out.

Through conditioning, you can be in a place of gratitude. You can see and feel your life through a different perspective. It will be easier to overcome any hurdles that may stand in your way.

Human beings, by default, tend to focus on the negative, which makes it even more important to train yourself and put yourself in a place of gratitude on a daily basis. By developing a daily practice, you will begin to pay attention to things that are important to you, and that's when you will start to claim your ultimate potential.

By practising gratitude for a few minutes each day, you can change your brain. You can increase your

GRATITUDE AND APPRECIATION

confidence in yourself to claim your ultimate potential. You will start to feel fantastic, and feelings are nothing more than an awareness of the vibration, the energy that flows through your body. By practising gratitude, you will be placing yourself in a positive state of mind.

When you feel gratitude, you also strengthen the circuits in your brain that are responsible for moral decision-making. You will help your children, your family, and everyone else around you.

Research has shown that business people who practise gratitude have more patience, and are not as materialistic as those who don't spend much time counting their blessings. Even someone who is depressed or stressed will strengthen the part of the brain that gives them the power to improve their behaviour. People who practise gratitude are more resilient, happier and healthier, and they have the ability to ask for help.

If you're struggling with something and the specific emotions and feelings that are associated with it, take a piece of paper and start writing down what you feel grateful for. This action will start to release feel-good chemicals in your body. If you stay in a place of worry and stress, however, different chemicals will be released. When you write down what you feel grateful for, those negative feelings will melt away, releasing the feel-good chemicals in your body. So make the time to put something down on paper.

You can also do a mental exercise. When you're thinking of something negative, close your eyes and release that thought. See yourself moving towards what you actually want. By doing this, you're teaching your brain how to overcome something that is negative you're expressing through your emotions. You're actually teaching your brain to look at something in a different way, a positive way.

When you feel gratitude, focus on what you've done rather than what you need to do. Celebrate and acknowledge yourself for what you have done, as well as what others have done for you. Acknowledge yourself for your capabilities, strengths, qualities, uniqueness, and what you bring to the world. Ask yourself who in your life lights you up when you feel down. Be grateful that person is in your life.

Develop a practice of waking up every morning with a smile on your face. This will release feel-good hormones in your body. Every single day you wake up, you can choose to be happy. Smile, even though you may wake up uncomfortable or with aches and pains. Take the time to be aware of and grateful for all the things that

GRATITUDE AND APPRECIATION

are working in your life. You will have more energy to focus on the things that are not working as well. Look at the things that empower you, that inspire you.

This is a skill that you can learn. It's a tool that you can use, just as you learned how to drive a car. You can direct your attention towards gratitude, and you will find even more things to be grateful for. Being in a place of gratitude means you will feel thankful for everything in your life.

Being grateful can transform a day of stress into a day of fulfilment so you can claim your ultimate potential. Being in a place of gratitude is the secret to fulfilment.

Stop and reflect on your day-to-day activities. Be grateful for the events, people and opportunities that are present in your life, and that you experience on a regular basis. When you do, you will find yourself looking at things from a different perspective. Most successful people have this ability. They can transform any stressful situation because they come from a place of gratitude.

Having grateful thoughts will empower you to make better decisions. You will feel better within yourself. You will open up your heart, and that will allow you to feel present, to be in the moment.

Writing down your thoughts and feelings, especially what you're grateful for, and being present in that moment, will give you a sense of fulfilment. You will notice that you feel far happier because writing things down will allow you to gain more clarity and focus on what's important. Zig Ziglar said, 'Gratitude is the healthiest of human emotions. The more you express gratitude for what you have, the more likely you will have even more to express gratitude for.' Every evening, ask yourself what you feel grateful for. You will go to sleep with a smile because you will be focusing on positive things.

Now that you have been introduced to so many different options, it's important to pick what resonates with you, and then develop a morning and evening practice to fit your individual needs and your lifestyle. Your practice, whatever it is, will bring you fulfilment, joy, and a sense of satisfaction when you commit to it and when you do it consistently. Even a few minutes will be better than nothing. The most important thing is to be committed, because when you're committed to something you will make the time to ensure that you do it.

If the thought of adding yet another thing to your day makes you feel stressed, just start with ten or fifteen minutes and build up from there. You can sit down anywhere to meditate, read your affirmations, or

GRATITUDE AND APPRECIATION

visualise your goals. The important thing is that you schedule specific and dedicated time for yourself each day.

Like any healthy habit, your morning and evening practices will work best if you're committed to them and do them on a regular basis. You could make it easier by finding an accountability partner and commit to a thirty-, sixty- or ninety-day challenge. An accountability partner will help you stick with your commitment.

We all have days when we intend to exercise but don't because we just don't feel like it. If you have an accountability partner who is willing to team up with you, you will feel more motivated. Studies have shown that we are more likely to follow through on something if another person holds us accountable for our behaviour. You and your accountability partner can hold each other accountable to make sure you both stay on track.

When you go to bed, think about what you have to look forward to the next day. Are you meeting with a special friend? Are you looking forward to a delicious coffee or breakfast? Finding reasons to be excited about the next day will make it a lot easier to get up in the mornings.

In *The Power of Habit*, Charles Duhigg explains how the ingrained habits that are in our lives, such as

YOUR TIME IS NOW

brushing our teeth, smoking or exercising, are formed. Which practice will you choose to include in your life? Start with one and build from there. The secret is consistency.

Now you know the secret: the answer to achieving a successful, fulfilling life and claiming your ultimate potential lies in your morning and evening practices together with taking action towards what you love to be, do, have and give. Give yourself permission to experience life fully and committee to yourself as this is your time; your time is now to claim your ultimate potential.

You are the universe you're experiencing, and the magic you seek ... is you!

—SHARON PEARSON

References

1. *12 Rules for Life: An Antidote to Chaos*, Jordan Peterson, 2018.
2. *Awaken the Giant Within: Take Immediate Control of Your Mental, Emotional, Physical and Financial Destiny*, Anthony Robbins, 2001.
3. *Becoming Supernatural: How Common People Are Doing the Uncommon*, Dr Joe Dispenza, 2017.
4. *Big Potential: Five Secrets of Reaching Higher by Powering Those Around you*, Shawn Achor, 2018.
5. *Change Your Thoughts Change Your Life: Living the Wisdom of the Tao*, Dr Wayne W Dyer, 2010.
6. *Decoding Your Client's Limits: Why Success Eludes Some People and What to Do About It*, Joe Pane, 2010.
7. *Disruptive Leadership: 4 Simple Steps to Creating the Winning Team*, Sharon Pearson, Global Success Institute Pty Ltd, 2015.
8. *Eat That Frog: Get More of the Important Things Done Today*, Brian Tracy, 2016.
9. *Feel the Fear and Do It Anyway*, Susan Jeffers, 2012.

10. *Flow: The Psychology of Optimal Experience*, Mihaly Csikszentmihalyi, 2008.
11. *From Stress to Success in Just 31 Days*, Dr John Demartini, 2015.
12. *How to get a bigger bite out of life! Power-packed ideas for personal growth & prosperity*, George Faddoul, 2011.
13. *Innercise: The New Science To Unlock Your Brain's Hidden Power*, John Assaraf, 2018.
14. *Keep Your Brain Alive: 83 Neurobic Exercises to Help Prevent Memory Loss and Increase Mental Fitness*, Dr. Laurence C. Katz, Pg.D., & Manning Rubin, 2014.
15. *Lead the Field*, Earl Nightingale, e-book, Nightingale-Conant, 2014.
16. *Learned Optimism: How to Change Your Mind and Your Life*, Martin EP Seligman, PhD, 2006.
17. *Man's Search For Meaning*, Victor E. Franks, 2004.
18. *Mind to Matter: The Astonishing Science of How Your Brain Creates Material Reality*, Dawson Church, 2018.
19. *Mindset: Changing the Way You Think to Fulfil Your Potential*, Dr Carol S Dweck, Robinson, 2012.
20. *Secrets of the Millionaire Mind: Think Rich To Get Rich, Mastering the Inner Game of Wealth*, T. Harv Eker, 2005.
21. *Simple Strategies for Business Success: How to WIN at the Game of Business and Live Life on YOUR Terms!*, Sharon Pearson, The Coaching Institute, 2010.

REFERENCES

22 *Sleep Smarter: 21 Essential Strategies to Sleep Your way to a Better Body, Better Health and Bigger Success*, Shawn Stevenson, 2015.
23 *Sleight of Mouth: The Magic of Conversational Belief Change*, Robert B Dilts, 1999.
24 *The 3rd Alternative: Solving Life's Most Difficult Problems*, Stephen R Covey, 2012.
25 *The 5 Seconds Rule: Transform your life, work, and confidence with everyday courage*, Mel Robbins, 2017.
26 *The 7 Habits of Highly Effective People: Powerful Lessons in Personal Change*, Stephen R Covey, 2013.
27 *The 8th Habit: From Effectiveness to Greatness*, Stephen R Covey, 2005.
28 *The Brain That Changes Itself: Stories of Personal Triumph from the Frontiers of Brain Science*, Norman Doidge, MD, 2017.
29 *The Breakthrough Experience: A revolutionary New Approach to Personal Transformation*, Dr John F Demartini, 2002.
30 *The Future of the Body: Exploration into the Further Evolution of Human Nature*, Michael Murphy, 1992.
31 *The Magic of Thinking Big*, David J Schwartz, PhD, 2012.

32 *The Miracle Morning: The 6 Habits That Will Transform Your Life Before 8 a.m.*, Hal Elrod, Hodder and Stoughton, 2016.
33 *The Now Habit at Work: Perform Optimally, Maintain Focus, and Ignite Motivation in Yourself and Others*, Neil A Fiore, PhD, 2010.
34 *The Power of Habit: Why We Do What We Do and How to Change*, Charles Duhigg, 2012.
35 *The Power of When: Discover Your Chronotype—and the Best Time to Eat Lunch, Ask for a Raise, Have Sex, Write a Novel, Take Your Meds, and More*, Michael Breus, PhD, 2016.
36 *The Power of Your Subconscious Mind*, Dr Joseph Murphy, 2006.
37 *The Universe Has Your Back: How to Feel Safe and Trust Your Life No Matter What*, Gabrielle Bernstein, 2015.
38 *The Values Factor: The Secret of Creating an Inspired and Fulfilling Life*, Dr John Demartini, 2013.
39 *Think and Grow Rich*, Napoleon Hill, The Ralston Society, 1938.
40 *Ultimate You: Quest Edition*, Sharon Pearson, 2018.
41 *What They Don't Teach You At Harvard Business School*, Mark H. McCormack, 2014.

REFERENCES

42 *Your Legacy Is Every Life You've Touched,* https://www.youtube.com/watch?v=af7u70yTf5s, accessed on 11.11.2017.
43 *Your Success: 10 Steps to an Extraordinary Life*, Sharon Pearson, The Coaching Institute, 2006.

YOUR TIME IS NOW

"Let your actions create a legacy that inspires others to dream more, learn more, become more and have more, and then and only then will you be an empowering leader."
—**Mariana Ardelean**

Notes

YOUR TIME IS NOW

NOTES

YOUR TIME IS NOW

Empowering Strategies

YOUR TIME IS NOW

Join in the conversation

www.facebook.com/marianaardeleanpage
www.marianaardelean.com
www.yourtimeisnow.com.au

Love to hear and connect with you

www.ingramcontent.com/pod-product-compliance
Lightning Source LLC
Chambersburg PA
CBHW071108160426
43196CB00013B/2505